THE HALF-ALIVE ONES

THE HALF-ALIVE ONES

Clinical Papers on
Analytical Psychology in
a Changing World

Eva Seligman

KARNAC
LONDON   NEW YORK

First published in 2006 by
H. Karnac (Books) Ltd.
6 Pembroke Buildings, London NW10 6RE

British Library Cataloguing in Publication Data

A C.I.P. for this book is available from the British Library

   ISBN 1 85575 374 X

Edited, designed and produced by The Studio Publishing Services Ltd.
www.publishingservicesuk.co.uk
E-mail: studio@publishingservicesuk.co.uk

Printed in Great Britain by Hobbs the Printers Ltd, Totton, Hampshire

www.karnacbooks.com

CONTENTS

For my sons David and Benjamin, and for Minky

ACKOWLEDGEMENTS

My gratitude to, and my appreciation of, Robin Daniels, who kept me in order and did all the foot work; to Jeff Bampton, who generously and efficiently provided me with all the means to my end; to Philip Gell, who imaginatively designed the book cover, and to Pat Ryan for her infinite patience.

Also to all those who follow their star.

Eva Seligman was born in Berlin in 1922 and immigrated to Great Britain with her family in 1933. During her medical studies she volunteered for the Air Force. Following her discharge, she studied Social Science and Mental Health at the London School of Economics, followed by work at the Maudsley Hospital and as a lecturer at LSE. Subsequently, she joined the Tavistock Institute of Marital Studies, beginning her analytical training in 1958.

She has been in private practice throughout and is a training analyst of the Society of Analytical Psychology. Eva Seligman is also a painter and a poet. A comprehensive collection of her poetry was published in 2002, entitled *The Cost of Loving*.

PREFACE

This eminently readable book distils much of the author's decades
of analytical and psychotherapeutic work. For many years she was
a senior therapist at the Tavistock Institute of Marital Studies, and
also a training analyst for the Society of Analytical Psychology and
a training psychotherapist for other psychotherapy training bodies
in England. Eva presents here a selection of clinical papers, most of
which were originally read at national and international conferences and later published in various professional journals. We are
given a refreshing and frank account of her humane and flexible
approach to analysis. Her case histories are particularly valuable in
illustrating how, in the development of the individual person,
nature and nurture, instinct and environment, the archetypal and
the personal, are in continual interaction in the building up of character and of the problems that lead our clients to seek help. It is
clear that the author has achieved a working balance, or rather an
integration, of these opposites, which is necessary if analysis is to
be a creative interaction, and the case histories clearly illustrate this
to be the case. The importance of the inner and outer mother, the
inner and outer father, and of the feeling tone of the internalized
relationship between them, comes through beautifully time after

time throughout the book. For example, by virtue of her long experience of analysis and her marital work, she shows how an emotionally absent outer father can result in an emotionally absent
inner father, and a consequent emotionally absent part of the self.

Two consequences of this integrated approach follow. One is the
absence of the counterproductive multiplicity of dos and don'ts,
rights and wrongs, which bedevilled, and still bedevils, the various
trainings in analysis and which result in so much anxiety and rigidity in our trainees, at least when they are used defensively, rather
than as useful rules of thumb. The other is the inclusion of accounts
of failed and partially failed therapy, which, as we know, are often
even more instructive than the successful examples.

We are indeed fortunate that Eva has been able to collect
together and present in such a readable and satisfying whole her
experience in the different areas of work she has enriched over her
professional lifetime.

Joseph Redfearn

We shall not cease from exploration
And the end of all our exploring
Will be to arrive where we started
And know the place for the first time.

[T. S. Eliot, "Little Gidding",
No. 4 of *Four Quartets*]

CHAPTER ONE

The case for a versatile approach to analytical practice

All insights are private and words but vehicles we use to convey the incommunicable. Yet we continue the attempts to pool information, hopeful of stimulating an interchange of ideas based on our own experience, and to learn from one another.

In this chapter I shall be describing adaptations in my own practice, which I believe to have evolved out of our changing civilization. These adaptations seem, to some extent, to lie outside the mainstream of analytical practice and, moreover, require a highly diversified approach from patient to patient that cannot readily be accommodated within our traditional conceptual framework. My account naturally has a subjective, if you like an autobiographical, side to it; and here I take courage from the following lines in Jung's *Memories, Dreams, Reflections:*

> I am often asked about my therapeutic or analytical method. I cannot reply unequivocally to the question. Therapy is different in every case. When a doctor tells me that he adheres strictly to this or that method, I have my doubts about his therapeutic effect. . . . Psychotherapy and analysis are as varied as are human individuals. [Jung, 1963]

1

To begin with I should like to make four points, which I shall afterwards illustrate with case material.

First, I should like to emphasize the effects on the analyst of the consequences of the very considerable growth in psychological information to which the public has access through mass media. Never before have ordinary people been so assailed, in countless publications, by psychological topics, frequently slanted, often tendentious, and regurgitated by questionable sources. As a result, far too many people assimilate what passes for psychological knowledge in a way that promotes confusion rather than genuine understanding. As regards treatment, the widespread sedating and tranquillizing of patients, together with the extensive consumption of mind-bending drugs, more often than not merely glosses over the reason for the mental pain and conflict, producing perhaps some improvement in functioning for a time, but yielding little insight into the *meaning* of those symptoms.

These phenomena do little to lessen the ever-escalating isolation of the individual. At the same time they contribute towards a growing demand for some form of psychotherapeutic help. Consequently, available resources are severely stretched. Fortunately, minimal intervention can often bring about a real change for the better in a serious crisis. I cannot see how analytical psychologists can afford to turn their backs on this situation.

Second, I shall pay attention to the fact that my current practice is increasingly shifting towards younger patients, chronologically in their twenties and thirties, but all the same greatly concerned not only with acquiring an identity, but also searching, as it were, for the discovery of their true selves. My experience of working with many people in the first half of life bears out Michael Fordham's views on individuation as a continuing process throughout the whole span of a lifetime (Fordham, 1969). The more traditional model of a predominantly reductive analysis of young people seems to me no longer adequate to the understanding of the present-day generation. It omits an important therapeutic ingredient. Jung referred to it when he wrote: "Every trace of routine can prove to be a blind alley" (Jung, 1933).

Third, I am of the opinion that I rarely work with a single patient who is ill by himself. I find it more fruitful to perceive him and to treat him as part of a total situation, which he brings alongside of himself. This approach, while making use of the well-tried tools of analysis, requires other, less well-documented avenues that reach beyond the more familiar two-person analytic set-up. I have therefore deliberately refrained from referring to transference phenomena.

Fourth, I maintain that economic considerations in their widest sense, i.e., the energy and time resources of both analyst and patient as well as the financial situation, need to be given their rightful place. Geographical distances, for instance, can impose considerable restrictions. Although many patients are, of necessity, willing to travel for hours, they must continue to earn a living and to care for their children. Therefore, unless a great many people, sometimes desperate, often well motivated and psychologically accessible, are to be turned away, the therapist must be prepared to make concessions. Mindful of the analyst's limitations as well as the patient's inner and outer resources, I am in favour of remaining flexible. The cutting of corners, whether it is by necessity or by choice, can and does have its therapeutic value. Indeed, I should like to go further and state with conviction that a more directive and reality-testing type of therapeutic approach is no mere indulgence, nor an aberration from analytical procedures, but rather an unavoidable and necessary development.

No one will dispute the fluidity of our present social structure, with its permissive climate; this pattern is bound to be reflected in current practice. By and large, I now feel more comfortable with the doors of my mind and of my room sufficiently ajar to admit the third, the inseparable other to accompany the patient at a given moment in time. It may turn out to be a tape-recording of a young patient on an LSD trip, brought by him in the vain hope of some profound revelation. Only in his subsequent replaying of the tape will he convince himself of the futility of an LSD-saturated session. More frequently, I have found myself confronted with the unplanned and unsolicited appearances of a spouse, of the baby or of unmanageable children, of a beloved dog, and also the frantic parent of an adult patient.

These more flexible techniques, which I now favour with certain of my patients, seem to me to concur with the spirit of Jung's writing and with his practice. To quote one passage picked at random: "Each case is individual and not derivable from any preconceived formula. Each is a new experiment of life in her ever-changing moods, and an attempt at a new solution or new adaptation" (Jung, 1926).

This does not mean that I have abandoned the basic structure of analytical procedures. I have tried to vary and develop them, but continue to learn from them and how best to apply them. The cases I present will show that it would be difficult to accommodate more than a limited number. I am attempting a fresh approach to my work. Such patients tend to be very demanding in their way, spuriously coming up with surprises that impinge on timetables, plans, and the furniture. This work, though initially based on hunches and conjectures, is reinforced by one's capacity to understand the *meaning* of the action; but it is not without risk. I am quite prepared to be drawn into aspects of a patient's outer life, as well as those of his inner self, and to share his most immediate burden; I will not, however, grant him entry into my private life. Some part of my own space remains sacrosanct.

I shall now give an illustration of a microscopic intervention, which seems to have been incisive in spite of the economy in time, money, and energy. This case might equally well have provided material for an extensive period of work, but circumstances decreed otherwise.

The prisoner

An unknown man with a Welsh accent rang me up. "I am a prison officer. I have a drinking problem which makes me violent towards my wife and child, and I am also in danger of losing my job." As I had two free hours, I asked him if he would come right away, which he did. He told me his life story. His father had died when he was two, and he had been surrounded and brought up entirely by women, who made him feel suffocated and restricted. He had begun his heavy, solitary drinking when, following the birth of his child, his married life had likewise become constricting and stifling. He felt as if he had lost his wife, who was taken up with the baby, and I linked this with the loss of his father: had father lived, he would have acted as a buffer against the suffocating women of his childhood. I further drew his attention to his attempt to come to grips with his inner predicament by working in a prison where others, not himself, were being deprived of their liberty. This situation could not but repeatedly bring him face to face with his inner-most problems, primary among which, after all, was that of feeling a prisoner.

I heard from him on three other occasions in all, each time by a tele-phone call made at night from a pub. I could hear the hubbub of the bar in the background. "I am about to get drunk again, but I don't want to." We had a longish talk, elucidating which recent event or experi-ence had triggered off his flight to the bottle. On the first two occasions, the conversation ended with his saying: "I am all right now. I am not going to get drunk. I shall go home." Some weeks later he telephoned me for the last time. "I no longer drink. I wanted you to know that all is well. We are emigrating to Australia where a better job is waiting for me."

That was the end of the contact with this one man; but let me go back to Jung. I quote: "When we are dealing with the human soul, we can only meet it on its own ground, and this is what we have to do when we are forced with the real and overpowering problems of life . . ." (Jung, 1946).

Before I continue, I should like to explain that I tend not to make a decision about whether to take on a patient for analysis if I have any doubts as to whether analysis is the treatment of choice for a given individual. I usually see a new patient for several spaced-out weekly sessions prior to a commitment by either side.

So it was with "the tied-up man", my second example.

The tied-up man

He was a tall, handsome, young-looking forty-year-old, nonchalant and arrogant. He had been going on and off to analysis with a male analyst who had, quite simply, got fed up with him. His irregular sessions had spanned several years. He was unmarried, and always had been. To some extent he was bi-sexual, falling in love as he did with beautiful young men. However, he also liked playing with girls.

I felt he was intent on intimidating me by his overbearing, presumptu-ous manner, and he seemed to be trying to play games with me, too. By far the most exciting of these games was that of getting a woman to tie him up, if not in fact, then, at least in fantasy. For him this was the ultimate thrill and triumph. He boasted that he belonged only to his mother as he always had, and it became clear to me that he would use his analyst as a camouflage which would allow him to perpetuate this condition indefinitely.

In his sixth session he spoke with enthusiasm about T. S. Eliot's *Four Quartets* (Eliot, 1940). They had been broadcast recently; I had heard them, and been moved by them too. Then I remembered Eliot's words: "In my beginning is my end", and later: "what we call the beginning is often the end. And to make an end is to make a beginning . . ." I took my cue from these lines: without any clear, prior decision the situation with this patient had fallen into place, and I realized that this was to be our last session. I proceeded to explain the reasons to him as follows: he was seeking experiences that would ultimately not change anything but only enable him to hold on to the symbiotic mother whom he had never renounced. I could see that the prospect of cutting the tie with his mother would constitute his renunciation of her magical powers, which he could not yet do without. He made them a part of himself. So I told him if he was ready to tackle this struggle in earnest, he could come back. He went away feeling relieved, perhaps because he had for once encountered a woman who declined to tie him up.

I have recently heard by chance that he is more content with life. I think that whatever was possible at that point in time was achieved and that a long-drawn-out attempt to analyse him would have been sabotaged by him.

My third case links with the idea that only rarely do I work with a single patient who is ill by himself.

Mother with Anna

A woman in her thirties has been in analysis with me for about two years. She has two abortive marriages behind her, and she is frigid with her third husband, a man old enough to be her father, who treats her and even dresses her like a precious doll. My patient has a narcissistic personality, suffers from phobias and hysterical conversation symptoms. Each night she goes through an acute attack of terror, convinced that she is going to die. She is capable of persuading herself that she has the symptoms of every known fatal disease. She also has an eating disturbance, and alternates between gorging herself and starving. Her weight has oscillated between twelve stones and seven. She was an only daughter, and her mother's "divine child". She remembers with horror how her mother devoured her with her eyes. Her father was always experienced by her as old, weak, pathetic, and disgusting.

One day, without warning, my patient came with Anna, her only daughter, aged three, clinging on to her. Anna, like mother, was dressed immaculately like a doll, but all skin and bones, furtive, waif-like. Mother was in one of her starvation phases, and said she had brought Anna because Anna would not eat. "You have brought a bit of yourself as a three-year-old," I said to her.

We encountered a double repetition here. The husband treats my patient as her *own* mother had, and she in turn does the same to Anna, who is already displaying similar symptoms; Anna also had difficulties in falling asleep, like mother.

To continue with the session: Anna now placed herself strategically between her mother and myself, climbing all over mother like a baby monkey, demanding her unqualified attention, and preventing any communication between mother and me. I am spellbound by what the two of them are enacting. They hypnotize one another with their eyes and are totally absorbed with each other.

Nevertheless, at an unguarded moment Anna's eyes wandered to a corner of my room where she saw a bowl of fruit. Gradually, she disentangled herself from her mother, and stealthily propelled herself towards the fruit. Mother became tense, watchful, and anxious. I said, "Let her be." Slyly, with one eye fastened on mother, Anna began to pick at the fruit and became absorbed in eating it, by then quite oblivious of mother, who was talking to me freely. At that moment the grip of exclusive participation between mother and child had loosened.

I talked to my patient about her child's, as well as her own, need to achieve some separate existence, and linked their mutually shared entanglement with that which had existed between herself and *her* mother. I reminded her of her ambivalent feelings and resultant guilt towards both her mother and Anna. She hated and resented them both and tried to compensate with stifling closeness. She then confessed to her habitual compulsive need to tell the three-year old Anna *everything*, quite indiscriminately.

In the meantime, Anna was enjoying herself in her own way. She came and went to the fruit bowl, explored my room, ignored the toys mother had brought and invented her own games. She discovered a low chair and clambered on to it. Having always been very timid, she eyed her mother as before, but mother was now absorbed in herself. Anna became more enterprising, culminating with her leaping off the chair accompanied by cries of joy and release. They both left reluctantly. Anna no longer clung, but skipped up the path ahead of mother. Her subsequent session continued as before; my patient reported that Anna's eating had become less fitful, and that she herself was keeping to a normal diet.

The two of them came together a few more times, always without prior notice, and for all kinds of different reasons. Anna was filling out, and had become more venturesome. She always made straight for the low chair, which, clearly, she regarded as her own place.

It then became obvious that my patient was making a habit of bringing Anna to the last session before each holiday break. We discussed this emotional exploitation of her child, and her use of Anna as a shield against her own anxieties, just as her own mother had used *her*.

Mother and child were by now on the way towards something of a separate existence. Mutual enjoyment had largely replaced the hatred and resentment for which she compensated by over-identification. In the past, this had always been the pattern of relating.

I surmise that these developments would have taken much longer, and perhaps not happened at all, had Anna not personally participated.

My next case links with my fourth point, i.e., the impact of reality factors on the analyst's pattern of work.

The puppet woman

It all began with a long-distance telephone call from a frantic husband. His wife, he said, had slipped into her third bout of depression. She was once again almost totally immobilized; he went on to tell me that they have young children, and that he was a very busy professional man; they were desperate. In spite of heavy medication and ECT her condition was deteriorating. He had spent all day contacting analysts in London, and, since he and his family live a day's journey away, he had been advised to move all of them to London so that his wife could have analysis. Such a complete uprooting, however, seemed to him impracticable. He was just establishing himself professionally, and as a young family in their first house they were heavily committed financially, and already in debt.

I was uneasy about treating someone so ill at such a distance, but suggested that he ask his wife to write to me. After receiving her letter, written immediately, I felt that anything at all that might ameliorate her condition and the family situation would be worth a try. She had stressed in three places in her letter that, though she was only thirty-three, her life was over. I wondered whether her real age might not be nearer three. I was in no way prepared for who was to come—a thin, droopy woman without any affect, noticeably slowed down and slurred in her speech, and with a stiffening of her right leg and back which made her movements appear puppet-like, jerky, and grotesque. She half crawled, half shuffled into my room like a ninety-year-old; however, she had managed the long journey. Her non-verbal appeal was "help me"; it seemed probable that she was plagued by hysterical conversion symptoms. She gave me as much of the history of the illness as she was able and we explored the possibility of therapy. We eventually agreed she should have a thorough physical examination first, which, as expected, yielded no evidence of organic disease, and that the patient's illness was a desperate last stand to evoke a spark of love and caring from her mother, but she had drawn a blank, and so her illness had increased in severity to the point of near immobility.

I made use of such pointers as she provided. I put it to her that her depressive illness might stem both from her acute grief about her mother's coldness and from her unexpressed but intense hatred with its accompanying guilt. At this she blazed into life, raving against both her parents, ranting, cursing, and swearing with complete abandon. When she had become calmer, I simply said that she was now in touch with her *real* feelings, and might not need to be quite so ill any more. When she returned a week later, her physical symptoms had disappeared. She became noticeably less depressed, more lively, and dispensed with medication. The total duration of her treatment was eight months.

Though a kindly, generous and likeable person, she did not possess great depth. I set my sights low from the start, concentrating mainly on restoring her belief in herself and, most importantly, at re-establishing some measure of reconciliation with her mother. I hoped to help her envisage a future that would extend beyond her domestic life. She had been an academic failure at school. With some encouragement, she enrolled for "O" level classes, doing her studying and homework on her long train journeys. Subsequently, I have received a glowing letter from her; she had amazed herself by passing all of her subjects, and she was contemplating new pastures.

In retrospect, I am clearer about the way that reality problems can be harnessed as *allies* rather than be allowed to remain obstacles. Further, that the crucial decision for the analyst must be whether to build on the existing ego strength, however slender, or whether to aim at analysing and reducing faulty defences and to undertake a much more radical procedure.

In this particular case, I selected the former, acknowledging and working *with* the tide of limiting factors. The patient and I were therefore able to adapt to them.

Most psychological encounters have inconclusive endings; unequivocally positive results remain suspect, since frustration and disillusionment are integral to all human life. So my last two cases had ambiguous and problematical endings. Both these young patients were demanding and disturbing, at times exasperating, and both broke through the barriers of the safe walls of my consulting-room.

The flower growing through concrete

Linda had come to London from overseas on an impulse and relapsed, all alone, into yet another episode of paranoid schizophrenia.

When she contacted me, she had not been out of her one small rented room for three months. A sympathetic neighbour had provided her with the bare necessities of life. She looked deathly white, drab, thin, and had a mask-like, expressionless face. She described herself as a "twenty-four-year-old baby". She had been married once, for just one week. She called herself "ugly and hopeless". "I am," she said, "fastened on to a huge umbilical cord. I am washed about like a sea. Life is a room you never get out of. There is no boundary except death, which is definitive. I have never existed except through my mother. When she left home I was twelve, and I disintegrated."

More often than not Linda was deluded and hallucinated. She insisted that she could not leave her room because everyone would talk about her and she would be pursued by the police, who would put her away. She had, in actual fact, been several times tricked against her will by her father and stepmother into being committed to a psychiatric hospital. I felt she may need to go into hospital again, just to keep alive, and, though I did not relish the prospect, I arranged a bed for her that was kept available against the possibility of it being needed.

The first big hurdle was how to get her to my house, as she could not go out. The initial session was by telephone. Long silences interspersed with a plan of campaign. I would see her after dark, when she *felt* she could not *be* seen. She would order a taxi from door to door, and back again. She started to come. At first, whenever her session had ended, I had to leave her on her own in another room, and carry on with my work. Then, when she had gathered herself together, she would telephone for a taxi, and let herself out when it arrived. She came every day; she could not have managed a break. She would repeatedly say: "I am not here, and can't *go* anywhere." When not deluded, she would ask me astute, searching questions on any number of topics, including herself and her past. I always gave her a straight answer. I did not make a single interpretation of an as-if type; she could not have taken it. She needed maximum contact with reality.

Gradually, her spells of being *herself*, inside her own body, of her *existing in the world*, grew. She asked for a daytime appointment, and would wait for her taxi outside in the street instead of indoors. She painted her room, which had been stark white, she began to go shopping, she bought herself a camera, pretty clothes, her face became mobile. She unfolded like a flower. She then elected to *walk* the two miles to and from my house in bright daylight, all lit up and smiling, and bringing an over-size shopping basket. Her hallucinations still broke in spasmodically, but she was no longer sure whether she believed them.

Then she flew away, literally. She booked herself a seat on a plane to an exotic island, paid her rent, paid me, and was gone.

I knew her for just three months. I was left fearing that her fragile eggshell ego would crack with the first small knock, and then the flower would wilt in the concrete.

My last case typifies, to me, the young generation caught up in our changing pattern of civilization, and the plight of the analyst who finds himself being unavoidably dragged into all kinds of crises outside the sessions while attempting to hold on to his own ground.

The butterfly trapped in ice

Peter, whose own poignant description of himself this is, was the youngest of a long string of children, and came to England at eighteen to "escape", as he put it, "the achievement-orientated Western ego trip", and to create the greatest possible distance between himself and his parents' values and lifestyle that he abhorred. But, as it turned out, he also came to find his true self. When he started analysis at twenty-three, he had already traversed all the dark places frequented by the youth of today, hoping to fill his emptiness in the middle while struggling to obey current taboos on dependence. Characteristically, Peter looked like Jesus, with his long hair and his John Lennon glasses and his aesthetic features. He had an inappropriate childish smile when his feelings were stirred, which he called his "plastic laugh", intended to forestall *his* being laughed at by others. He was forever spinning beautiful pipe-dreams, to compensate for, and deny his ruthless self-destructive drive. He was steeped in the drug scene, and in homo-sexual and heterosexual yearnings. He had worshiped at the shrines of psychedelics, encounter groups, communes of every persuasion, and the rest. He was a night creature, like so many of his contemporaries, seeking to transcend the temporariness of their existence by huddling up together with other drifting spirits in shady holes and corners.

It was clear that Peter needed a pivot to his life, and a firmly holding yet responsive set-up. I arranged to see him five times a week, some-times more, and deliberately in the early morning whenever possible, for he needed some reality-based impetus to propel him out of his formless way of life. He always turned up, at first frequently tripping or otherwise drugged, or from a few hours' sleep snatched on some-one's anonymous floorboards. He was always running, irrespective of whether he was early or late. People like him defy the clock, feeling pursued by what they have put off, or left unfinished, or have never begun at all.

Peter was adept at building fantasy castles everywhere, isolating himself in them. He was obsessed with the imaginary freakishness of his body, which he deliberately neglected in order to oppose his father, who had pushed him into developing his muscles and athletic prowess. He was stunted by guilt, his mother having told him throughout his childhood that he was driving her to suicide. His nearest brother, after a series of deliberate car crashes, finally succeeded in getting himself killed, and as Peter had hated him, he felt that he had killed his brother.

He was also overcome with feelings if inadequacy, though by the skin of his teeth he had just about managed to obtain a university degree. His mother wanted *him* to achieve all that *she* had failed in, so he complied by being a smart kid. As he said, he *pretended* to be clever, thus arousing his older brothers' envy and attacks; to survive, he then became weak and sneaky, and he hated himself for this. He dared not let anyone know that he had something of his own to offer. "I was either God," he said, "or a worthless swine, never a human being. I shouldn't ever have been born!" He distorted situations so as to make himself appear either an impotent nobody or, with his child-like incessant talk, an inflated megalomaniac capable of unlimited destruction or achievement. His eventual downfall was due to his abortive attempts to manipulate reality to conform to *him*. He deceived himself into believing that he was a crusader with a mission to enlighten the world. He ended up, predictably, as the one who was always being crucified.

Nevertheless, his analysis was making inroads on his innermost conflicts, and once when he had gone off taking drugs, he said: "Analysis is like climbing a mountain. You have to do the trudging and cannot stand still." His intense repressed attachment to his mother became prominent, as did his longing for her unconditional love, and for a father with whom he could have identified. At the same time, he was craving for, and steadily pursuing, the fulfilment of his own personality, heroically challenging his dragons, the devouring mother, and the weak father who betrayed him and had "thrown him to the wolves", as he put it.

Once only, out of an unconscious rebellion, he had had a homosexual love affair, which had in truth not severed his incestuous parental bonds. When it broke up, he had made a serious suicide attempt. His former submissive self reasserted itself: his confidence in his capacity to give and accept love was shaken. When we came to discuss this suicide attempt, which had taken place before he came into analysis, he clearly recognized it as a symbolic return to the womb, in the same way as his LSD trips had been. He also came to recognize that he *had* to fall so that his mother would pick him up, and to create emergencies so that *she* would rise to them.

In the session preceding his arrest, Peter brought me an expensive picture of a barren tree surrounded by desolate, crumbling buildings. He had stolen it, but had signed it with *his* name, an exercise in self-deception. He said that the picture depicted death; to me it felt like a premonition of disaster. He wanted to give it to me, but I did not accept it.

That night, he was picked up by the police, and subsequently remanded in prison. There, he faced many bitter truths and painful but invaluable insights. Both he and his mother from far off put pressure on me to act as *locum parentis*, and they tried to persuade me to stand bail for him. After a struggle with myself I wrote to Peter in prison to tell him that though I would not be his surrogate mother and bail him out, I would keep his analytical times for him in spite of his requests that I should fill them. I felt this was something of an initiation rite; with the *infantile* part of himself he felt abandoned by me, accused me of callousness and lack of concern. With his more adult side, however, he was experiencing the consequences of his own actions; when he eventually came back into analysis he was somewhat more integrated.

At this point, his mother entered the scene, arriving unexpectedly together with Peter's only sister and her young baby. His mother sensed a confrontation and had provided herself with two bodyguards.

Peter carried on with his own sessions, but we also met in a variety of combinations, from all five of us, to mother/sister/Peter/me; and then, most significantly, we had several meetings of Peter and myself *with* his mother. I also saw his mother on her own a few times. Ostensibly, she had come to visit him, but in truth, she and he were both ready to cut the cord, and for her to retrieve and own the part of their shared illness that belonged to *her*. This crucial task was accomplished. She shed her moralistic condemnatory attitude of her son, whom she had accused of "conning" *her* by breaking the law. With suffering and with relief, she exposed her own problems, most of all her inexhaustible appetite for unconditional love or its nearest substitute, food. Her enormous bulk had been a constant source of embarrassment to Peter. She admitted, and lived through her despair at feeling discarded and exploited by her large family. She came to understand herself and therefore to accept her failings, particularly her need to overpower and manipulate others, her excessive greed and acquisitiveness, and her tendency to get ill in order to evoke love. She ceased blaming Peter and projecting her failings and expectations on to him. When she departed, both Peter and his mother had acquired boundaries within which they could come to grips with what belonged to each of them.

Peter gained greater freedom in the midst of uncertainty and a welter of other police charges pending against him. He seemed nearer to achieving his own selfhood, more separate, less alone. He began to do creative and productive work.

Then came the bombshell: a deportation order. With much effort on my part, this order was eventually changed so that he was given a postponed date by which he would have to leave the country, and he was not to return for three years. The postponement provided him with valuable time to work through his separation crisis with me. On the eve of his departure he left four objects with me: a book with the optimistic title *I'm O.K. You're O.K.*, Jung's *Psychological Reflections* with the title page painstakingly engraved by him in a multi-coloured mandala with Jung's name at the centre; a plant that, he explained, grows towards the light, and an unfinished painting of his mandala without a centre. "I will finish it when I return in three years," he said.

By way of summary and conclusion, I would like to stress that aspect of my practice which came out most clearly in the case of Peter as well as in the case of "mother with Anna", i.e., the actual participation of the third person in the therapeutic sessions. This seems indicated when an intensive unconscious enmeshment with the third is the major content of a patient's life, and thus constitutes the main psychopathology of his illness. The two of them may have established between themselves an encapsulated autonomous unit, fortified by mutual projections of their own personalities and producing a state of fusion or false-self complex. The cohesive strength of that complex may be such that analytic interpretations are blocked off or bounced back without any noticeable impact. Two people may be so closely interlocked that a change cannot be brought about in either of them quite separately; they are *not* separate. My experiences have convinced me that a transformation can best be initiated when the two persons are brought face to face in the presence of the analyst, who recognizes the inner needs of *each* in his own right. They find themselves in a new reality situation in which they have never met before, and which enables them to perceive the other more objectively while at the same time gaining insight into their own problems. The therapist in such cases acts as the catalyst. By adopting a versatile approach, therefore, minimal intervention by the analyst together with the inclusion of the symbiotic partner can effect a new stage of integration that will further the development of psychic growth.

CHAPTER TWO

The half-alive ones

T his chapter was first conceived many years ago while working with my first-ever analytic patient, but it did not take
shape until 1980, when I was invited to give a lecture on the
topic at the University of British Columbia, Vancouver. I chose to
focus on the pattern of the parental marriage, with special reference
to the role of the father in personality formation. Furthermore, I was
unexpectedly asked to do two radio call-in programmes on the
same subject. A remarkable feature was that the lecture stimulated,
in the main, questions from separated and divorced members of the
audience concerned for their fatherless children. The radio callers
were exclusively either fathers at the point of separation from their
wives, desperate about the threatened loss of their children, or else
men who had taken on children who were not their own and who
were deeply troubled about whether these children would ever
accept them as their father.

As an analyst, I had been preoccupied with the inner world
of the patients who presented, and described themselves as "half-
alive", and I continued my search for some common denominators.
They appeared to dwell, as it were, in a state of permanent twilight, of non-differentiation, inexorably trapped. I remember an

extreme example, a woman recently divorced, suffering from an acute phobic condition, obsessed with a fear that the sun would never rise again, and that she would spend the rest of her life in everlasting darkness. In the course of her analysis it transpired that, on the one hand, she felt herself to be almost irresistibly pulled back into the powerful, but suffocating dark embrace of her mother, represented also by her husband, and on the other, she longed to come alive as herself, discovering and developing her own atrophied identity. It was an interminable tug-of-war. She came from a broken home and was effectively a fatherless child. Jung has pointed out that "the sun is a symbol of the source of life and the ultimate wholeness of man" (Jung, 1953). Gradually, my patient was able to relax into some measure of dependency without feeling smothered and suffocated and, with the diminution of her anxiety and of her fear of fragmentation, her own libido was liberated and she became able to construct a productive and creative existence for herself. During a holiday break early in her analysis, she wrote as follows: "I have allowed myself to become dependent, and my level of dependence will, I am sure, increase before it decreases. Only through developing an ability to acknowledge my dependency needs will I ever grow in the way that I want."

Before launching on the main subject matter, that is, the view I shall be putting forward that one of the main connecting threads in the "half-alive" patients is the "absence" of one parent—in my own cases more usually that of the father—a digression seems unavoidable. My North American experiences, together with a prolonged period doing marital work, have driven home the extent to which the realities of the modern world impinge forcibly on the analyst's foremost preoccupation, that of the life of the psyche.

Certain established facts cannot be ignored. For instance, the divorce rate for first marriages in North America exceeds even that in Britain, which is the highest in Europe, where countless fathers had been lost in two world wars. It has been calculated that three-quarters of divorces involve children under sixteen, many of them only babies or toddlers. The greater the acrimony, the less is the chance for the children of effectively keeping both parents. As yet, joint legal custody is only awarded in two and a half per cent of cases. Usually it is their father that children lose. Only a small number of them have any continuing contact with him during the formative childhood years.

It follows that, if the present trend of broken marriages continues, something over one million children over the next six years, in this country alone, will lose their father as if he had died, and perhaps, psychologically, in a more dangerous way than if he had (Thompson, 1981). These matters, however much they may give rise to concern, belong more appropriately to the province of the social scientist and cannot be dealt with here, but perhaps they are symptomatic of the matriarchal epoch into which we appear to have moved. I shall be confining myself to the significance, as I and others see it, of the symbolically "missing father". The next section will be concerned with the all-too-present mother. There is a strong connection between those two phenomena. I shall be referring to transference implications and intersperse the sections with clinical illustrations and a diagram, which is a pictorial representation of the vital configurations with parents that concern me here. I shall end by trying to show that the reinstatement of the father can be a potent factor in the development of personality. That reinstatement can take place in analysis through the transference.

The missing father

I need to make it clear that, when alluding to the missing father, I am referring to fathers *experienced* as unavailable both by the mother and by the child. In my cases he was physically present at least until the child's puberty, or beyond. If, then, the father is present, why is he being, or allowing himself to be, effectively obliterated? Is he being excluded or is he excluding himself? More likely than not, a combination of both factors is at work. First, I have evidence that there is an unconscious collusion between mother and child to maintain and prolong their mutually interdependent omnipotence and dependency in a dyad to satisfy one another's needs and wishes, thus postponing the more difficult and conflict-ridden subsequent phase of the triad, the phase of sharing and conflict. Second, as Layland (1981) points out: "Unresolved psychological problems in the father interfere with his role as a loving father". Furthermore, he draws attention to the evidence from the observations of Greenacre (1966), Abelin (1975), and Mahler, Pine, & Bergman (1975) that the infant has a sense of father from the early months of life: how much he remains a distant figure or what part he plays in his own right depends on his own temperament as well as that of the mother, and on the relationship between them. Abelin found that "a most definite turning towards the father occurs . . . at about the age of four months". Layland emphasizes the importance of the "father's own emotional response to the infant" and also the significance of "the father in supporting the mother in her mothering". These observations substantiate the most common reproach from the "half-alive" patients that their father did not support *them* either, in their attempts to emancipate themselves from their mother.

The all-too-present mother

Fordham (1971) states that "in essential respects the infant creates his mother in the light of his own needs and she therefore represents a part of the infant self". Newton and Redfearn (1977) draw our attention to Mahler's research, which demonstrates "the way in which the mother's feeling values, both conscious and unconscious, stimulate or inhibit her infant's potentialities". By the process of reconstruction in the analyses of the "half-alive" patients, the impression emerges of a large number of ego-damaging mothers, be they withdrawn, self-absorbed, or efficient but affectionless. Others were experienced as anxiously over-solicitous and over-protective, rigidly controlling, domineering and intrusive, or else seductive and castrating, puritanical and guilt breeding, or as tyrannizing their children by illness, more often feigned than real. There are martyred and dolorous mothers, others that cannot release a child, and those who exploit or scapegoat him. There are also the jealous mothers who vacillate between hostility and remorse. I can only conclude that the more unconsciously destructive the mother is, the less the child, even when he becomes an adult, can bear to be separated from her.

The missing father and the all-too-present-mother

As my clinical examples and the diagram (Figure 1) will show, I hope, the patient as a child was expected to conform to a high standard. The mother was usually seen as the stronger and more determined parent, whereas the father was perceived as the weakling. The mother, most particularly of only sons, was felt to be intensely ambitious beneath a show of martyrdom. The mother was presented as the moral authority, the child becoming cold and unloving, but fearful and desirous of approval. The father was thought of as weak and useless as a shield against the powerful mother and her phantasized revenge. Some fathers were experienced as siding with the mother or as indifferent and helpless. That would arouse anger and contempt in both mother and child, culminating in an exclusive mother–child "pair", which virtually shut out the father as a significant parent.

The rediscovery of the father

The remainder of this chapter will be concerned with my main thesis: the significance of the father in the formation of personality, which involves his rediscovery, as it were, within the therapeutic situation. Over and above that, it seems of paramount importance to effect the reconciliation of the parental imagos within the psyche, i.e., the reconciliation of the internalized parents. To support this proposition, I will be presenting clinical material. The names Stephen, Brian, Sheila, and Tom are all pseudonyms.

Stephen

Stephen came into analysis because he suffered from a host of debilitating psychosomatic symptoms. As a teacher, his worst afflictions were acute attacks of anxiety and panic that overcame him in crowded places, such as the daily morning school assembly. These attacks escalated into spells of giddiness, followed by vomiting and fears of fainting. Sometimes they were accompanied by blurred vision and uncontrollable, extended periods of hiccoughing. He came with utmost regularity, produced fascinating dreams and

Mother   Father   Son

Mother and Father
Together and Separate.
Child related to both,
To their union, and
Beginning to exist

1   as himself   Health

                                               Illness

Stephen
Father split off.
Mother and Child
Non-differentiated

2

Brian
Father, as the
Auxiliary parent
Accords with mother;
The son is barely
Half-alive

3

Tom & Sheila
All three unrelated
Leads to a yearning
To be re-incorporated
by a mother figure

4

Figure 1.

paintings, and his distress evaporated. After six months of analysis he concluded that he was "cured", and well enough to dispense with further treatment. Such "transference cures" should make us cautious and watchful because of the seductive, magical, almost numinous sensations that accompany them, and can infect both therapist and patient. They may lull the protagonists into an artificial sense of achievement and resolution. Stephen's intention to depart hastily was a warning signal that something alarming and painful was about to be uncovered. His defences were threatened, and his newly acquired but precarious equilibrium seemed to him to be at risk. Flight was his only escape. As Fordham (1980) states: "To infer fusion or paradisal bliss as a continuing state is an idealized phantasy". Had the sole goal and focus of his therapy been the relief of his symptoms, this might indeed have been the appropriate stage for stopping. But I realized that his attempt to retreat had been engendered by the positive, all too unambiguous transference relationship with me, which was about to close in on him, as had his mother's suffocating embrace. Newton (1981) refers to related themes: "An idealized love relationship . . . with its counterpart, a sado-masochistic opposite . . . a witch mother and a suffering victim child helpless in her clutches . . . illustrating a phase of ego immaturity and dependency". When I made an interpretation to him along those lines, his first dramatic anxiety attack in an analytic session occurred. Eventually, when he became calmer, he began to speak.

> "I am really a miserable fool who staggers and blunders about, and does not want to face anything. I am a pathetic, poor little one who cannot attack and who cannot be attacked. I experience phases of nothingness. Life is frozen, sexless, numb. I feel anonymous. Everything I have ever done was for someone else, to keep things just as they were. I have never done anything original in my life. My mother told me I was nearly suffocated at birth. I still am. I have travelled half way around the world [he had been in the Armed Forces], but I have never left my mother".

He had already told me that, throughout his school life, he would rather go through agony than use the school lavatories. His excreta were to be entirely preserved for his mother. Sometimes his acute discomfort had become so apparent that he had been sent home, thus also serving to alleviate his separation anxieties. At his demobilization camp, he claims not to have defecated for three weeks, at the end of which he was finally discharged home. When his mother had an eye operation, he had to stay off work because *his own* eyesight was so badly affected—a telling example of projective identification between a son and his mother. During two of her serious illnesses, Stephen developed identical physical symptoms, thus making it impossible for him to feel any concern for *her* at all. It was as if he had become so closely identified with her that the psychic and somatic boundaries between him and her had dissolved. Newton and Redfearn (1977) refer to "some psychosomatic states in which the parent's real body and the internalized mother's body are identical". In Stephen's case, an even more primitive process had occurred. He totally identified with his external mother's bodily states. Fordham (1971) speaks of infants in "states in which there seems to be fusion because the baby has not discovered how to distinguish between himself and the parts of his mother with which he comes into contact." Newton and Redfearn write on similar lines: "An inner situation of symbiosis when there are fluid boundaries between the sense of 'I' and 'other' ". I began to realize that the most important characteristic of the half-alive ones is their reluctance to relinquish the dependency, the close identification, and the deceptive sense of safety that are some of their distinctive features. The price they pay is imprisonment—a kind of death within life. Newton and Redfearn's apposite description is: "An iron circle tightening around emptiness". The afflicted participant is prepared to throw away almost everything of value that he has achieved for himself—in Stephen's case, his analysis, too—in order that he might preserve this imaginary state of "containment" to the bitter end. It had now become clear that this was Stephen's unconscious motive. The ostensible reason, that he was "cured", had deceived him. There can be no doubt that he was beginning to experience in his analysis and in the transference to his analyst the negative, suffocating aspects of his mother's choking embrace. The subsequent session confirmed those conjectures. He admitted that his analytic hours had become oppressive, suffocating, and inescapable. He now wanted to live his own life. Stephen further told me that he experienced sensations of suffocating most acutely during sexual intercourse with his wife. Newton and Redfearn (1977) refer to "shadow aspect of holding. The mother/self is devouring the infant/ego ... it represents a negative partnership". Stephen had brought with him a painting of a dark tree with overhanging, grasping, branches. When I commented that these branches looked like gripping arms, and that perhaps he felt they would crush him in a tight embrace, he was thrown into a panic, the second time it had happened in a session with me. Eventually, he muttered almost inaudibly that he could feel the branches suffocating and squeezing the life out of him. He then added that he was seeing me as a witch who could magically give him a good or an awful day—a characteristic of the archetypal great mother in her negative guise. I pointed out that this powerful witch was enshrined in his psyche and causing havoc in his inner and outer life; he could temporarily free himself of her by putting her outside of himself through projection on to me. I reminded him that he had been referred to me on account of his fears of suffocation, which were in conflict with his yearning to remain united with his mother for all time. I added that this reiterated request to stop seeing me, combined with the fact that he nevertheless continued to come, depicted the crux of his conflict. Much later on, he admitted that he had been intent on parting with me while all was still good between us, that is, while we were still as "one", and in no way a threat to one other. Subsequent sessions proved to be crucial, in that they enabled Stephen to resolve his ambivalence and to make a deeper commitment to analysis. Fordham (1971) attributed this development to the "modification of identifications developed in the course of maturation". Significantly, an upsurge of Stephen's masculinity occurred. He had the following dream:

"I was visiting my mother and father in different wards of a hospital. I said to them: 'Why can't you be together?' And then I set to moving their beds until they were side by side."

This dream marked the first mention of his father. Moreover, it revealed much concerning his vital childhood relationships. *Both* his internalized parents were in hospital; that is, emotionally sick in terms of Stephen's relationship to each of them, and theirs to each other. He had experienced them apart, and was now taking it upon himself to bring them closer together. This movement towards a reconciliation of the inner parents marked not only the beginning of the dissolution of his state of enmeshment with his mother but ushered in the subsequent reinstatement of his father as a potent figure in his inner life. The stranglehold on his psyche of the pre-Oedipal fixation on his mother was beginning to loosen. Outwardly, he became more enterprising. He had an engine fitted to his bicycle, and acquired a black leather jacket, which made him feel "more of a man". It had padded shoulders, big lapels, and gilt buttons. Nevertheless, he did not quite feel himself in it. The following dream occurred:

"I decided that my large black riding coat was too clumsy and did not allow me enough freedom of movement. I decided to cut it up, and to remake the coat in a different design. My mum and dad were both watching. I cut up the coat and experienced intense grief. It felt as if I had destroyed something of great value. Then I began laboriously to re-stitch the pieces, but this time it turned not into a coat but into a close fitting garment."

This dream confirmed Stephen's statement that he had not felt himself, that is, his true self, in the coat he had bought. Rather, he had attempted to acquire a pseudo- or false-self manliness, a camouflage for the as yet unresolved entanglement with his mother. The cutting up of the coat and its remaking into a close fitting garment symbolized a resurrection and rebirth of a truer identity. This dream tallied with developments in his analytic sessions and in his life. His personality became more clearly defined, less easily obliterated. Yet, with the growth and unfolding came the experience of grief and loss, stemming from the relinquishment of the primitive "fusion state", the surrender of idealizations, and the "depressive position". A short time later, Stephen began to refer to his father in more positive terms. With the unconscious aim of perpetuating their entwinement, Stephen and his mother had needed to see his father as useless and ineffectual. Together they had conspired to degenerate and dismiss the parental marriage as incompatible, so that Stephen might compensate his mother for the lack of satisfaction from her husband, her failed marriage. Thus, he recompensed her for an "absent" husband.

In my experience, half-alive patients more often than not have had half-alive mothers, unhappily married, who cling relentlessly to one or other of their children, projecting into this unfortunate child archetypal images of divinity or devilishness that smother the normal unfolding of the child's potential personality. As Newton and Redfearn (1977) point out: "Jung sees the personal mother as the first carrier of the archetype". These mothers are unable to combine a relationship, which simultaneously contains togetherness *and* separateness, and the ego development of the child becomes atrophied. They tend to relate to the growing child as if he were still a part of themselves, attached to their own bodies by the umbilical cord, so that he remains, in part, unborn. Prior to Stephen's request for help, he had left the parental home to marry the girl next door. They had set up house near his mother. The young couple spent all their free time doing identical things jointly, and Stephen described it as a "yes, dear, anything you like, dear" marriage. After some years, Stephen's wife went into hospital for her first and only confinement. During her absence of ten days, he became acutely anxious and feared that he was dying. His eyesight was blurred, he suffered from nausea, he was afraid that if he moved he would faint. According to his recollection, it was as if his legs would fold up under him; he felt utterly forlorn. I am well aware that I am describing classical hysterical symptoms, yet his condition takes on additional meaning, I feel, if perceived as a kind of developmental block, a defence against his wife's "otherness" and his being faced with the task of relinquishing the dyad.

A significant breakthrough occurred when his mother came to see the baby for the first time. She focused on the new arrival, and completely ignored Stephen. No longer was he number one for his mother, nor for his wife either. He felt so acutely cheated and irate that he rushed out of the room, overcome by murderous impulses towards his mother, his wife, and the child. He was both elated and terrified, and, at the same time, infused with an upsurge of energy. Change, for him, had ceased to be synonymous with death. During his wife's confinement, only two weeks earlier, he had not gone to work but lay in bed too terrified to move, or at best, sat huddled in a corner armchair. When his wife and baby girl subsequently returned home, he completely ignored the baby. His suffering was acute; her arrival had made him feel cast out. In his words, "someone turning away from me is like experiencing my own death". Stephen had been the youngest child in his family, and the only boy. His mother had restrained herself from becoming angry with him, nor had she ever punished him. When Stephen displeased her, her response had been, "Can't you see what you are doing to me?", implying that he was damaging her, further intensifying their psychological clinch. This response had effectively left him oblivious of the impact he could have on another person, because any unilateral action on his part was interpreted as destructive or damaging of his mother. Any minor digression left him with a load of guilt for having upset her. The extent and intensity of the attachment between himself and his mother had left no room for a relationship with his father, who had no existence for him.

This situation appears to be typical of the "half-alive" patients. As already stated, they insist on denying any experience of the father as a positive, effective figure in their own as well as in their mothers' lives. The "non-existent" father is indeed the most noteworthy common denominator in the personal history of these patients. It is the father, nevertheless, who plays a specific and essential role as the mediator of the difficult transition from the womb to the world. Without the father's emotional support, it seems to me that it becomes almost insurmountably difficult for a child to be properly born and confirmed in his own identity, and to negotiate the unavoidable separation from the mother, a prerequisite to a satisfactory adult heterosexual commitment. The "absent father" syndrome encourages a mutually collusive "embrace" with the mother, nourishing a shared illusion of "oneness", from which the developing child cannot extricate himself, leaving him neither in nor out of the womb, but wedged, so to speak, half-way, half-alive, half-born.

Earlier, I described Stephen as living in a state of twilight. When I looked up the word "twilight" in the *Oxford Dictionary*, I was surprised to find, among others, the following definition: "Twilight is a modern method of making childbirth painless". How apt! Birth is the first and most fundamental rupture, and of necessity accompanied by pain. To quote Jung: "Child means something evolving towards independence. This cannot be achieved without the child detaching itself from its origins; abandonment is therefore a necessary condition" (Jung, 1953).

The patients and mothers who concern me in this chapter have failed to negotiate even the first unavoidable separation, because neither child nor mother could tolerate the accompanying pain, feared deprivation, and sense of abandonment. The results have been pathological. It is my contention that the necessary separation requires the participation of the father. Yet, these mothers and their children are unconsciously intent on continuing to perceive the father as weak and useless, or else, as in my later examples, as violent and dangerous. There is an implicit prohibition on the growth of an openly warm and loving bond between father and child, because it does not exist between the parents either. It is noteworthy that Stephen, on his own initiative, opted out of taking an interest in his baby, thus also refuting the father *within*.

In these circumstances, a state of unnatural and ambivalent identification with the mother is prolonged. She is loved and has become indispensable, but surely she is envied for her power and over-competence, and possibly she is resented for her suffocating stranglehold and for her stressing of the mutual indispensability between the two of them. I hope to show that their unconscious interdependent needs are mutual, and, therefore, reversible. Either one may become the parent to the child within the other. This is by no means always recognized; too often, the problem is tackled only in the partner who presents the symptoms. Both, however, are burdened with acute dependency needs, alternating with sensations of being trapped and crippled, necessitating the erection of increasingly ridged and impenetrable defence systems that serve to camouflage weakness, dependence, and helplessness. It is just because of this unconscious imprisonment in an infantile state that these people fear, and consequently avoid, a new and different relationship, one that would present a challenge and demand a commitment. Their only apparent escape is to form the kind of bond that Stephen did in his marriage prior to the birth of their child, as close a replica as possible to the original mother–child bonding.

Transference implications

I have come to realize that in the initial phases of analysis in such a situation the patient seeks to establish a "fusion-like" mode of relatedness between himself and the analyst. I am sure that must be resisted. The truth lies in the contradiction, since the individuation process revolves primarily around conflict, the tension, and the integration of opposites. Creativity springs from the resolution and the reconciliation of opposing psychic forces within the individual.

The analyst's initial task is to establish a good enough therapeutic alliance with her patient so that basic trust is secured. Hopefully, the analyst's ego-boundaries are better established and more secure than those of the patient, and she is more conscious, more of a whole person, than the patient and his original partner. It is this that eventually facilitates the resolution of the *primary* "fusion" state. With that goal in mind, transference interpretations, which imply separateness between analyst and patient, however violently refuted by the latter, are crucial when the time is ripe. It is perpetually incumbent on the therapist to be aware of, and in touch with, the newly emerging personality that was formerly repressed. It must be remembered that any state of almost infantile dependence of one adult on another may ostensibly be wanted by the patient, but it is simultaneously humiliating and undermining. The patient actually knows, but likes to forget, the painful reality that he can never wholly possess or be possessed by his analyst or by anyone else. The conflict between the yearning for "oneness" and the opposite drive to reject it may engender a phase in the analysis when both participants become bogged down. Prolonged periods of passivity and hopelessness may have to be endured. Nothing appears to be happening and the analyst may come to feel that she has nothing to offer. Equally, the patient may feel worthless and inadequate, and he may become trapped in just *preserving* the analyst and the status quo. In Stephen's words, "it feels like disaster if anything were to change". People like him have impressed me with their infinite capacity to endure suffering without any awareness of the need, which also exists in them, to achieve satisfaction and happiness. Unable to relinquish the illusion of safety, which imprisons them, they appear to accept calmly a kind of death in life. Nevertheless, their frustration sooner or later catches up with them. Newton (1981) states it succinctly: "There is a loss of the illusion of 'oneness' and the inherent conflict of 'twoness' has to be sustained". Violent outbursts of rage and exaggerated recriminations ensue. I interpret this as a hopeful development, no matter how unpleasant it may be to find oneself at the receiving end! As a last stand, the patient may threaten to throw away everything, including his analysis, and perhaps even his life. Thus, he mistakenly hopes to ensure the preservation of "oneness" to the very end. The subject of my paper links with Jung's "The significance of the father in the destiny of the individual". To quote from the article in question:

> Freud has pointed out that the emotional relationship of the child to the parents, and particularly to the father, is of decisive significance in regard to the content of any later neurosis. This is indeed the infantile channel along which the libido flows back when it encounters any obstacles in later years, thus reactivating the long forgotten psychic contents of childhood . . . If the patient is a neurotic, he reverts back to the childhood relationships he has never quite forsaken, and to which the normal person is fettered by more than one chain—the relationship to father and mother . . . The source of the infantile disturbance of adaptation is naturally the emotional relation to the parents . . . The neurosis sets in the moment the libido is withdrawn from the infantile relationship, and for the first time comes a bit nearer to an individually determined goal . . .

The power which shapes the life of the psyche has the character of an anonymous personality . . . The parental imago is possessed of quite extraordinary power; it influences the psychic life of the child enormously. [Jung, 1961, para 728]

Stephen's material highlights, I believe, the role that the rein-statement of his father played in his analysis and, more importantly, in his life. Between us, we needed to enlist the help of his father, previously discarded and dismissed, yet having remained poten-tially vital and potent, so as to give Stephen sufficient security to relinquish his grip on his mother. With the start of the process, his conscious perception of his father began to alter, "I wonder if dad was ever *allowed* to be effective" or "I now think of dad as having been sucked dry by mother like a leech", he would say. His dreams continued to confirm his need of his father. In one of them, he was searching his father's waistcoat and found some valuable gold coins. In another, he went to his father for ammunition for his gun; that is, his father became the classical link with his own sexual potency. In a third dream, he climbed into bed beside his mother *and* father; in this bed, all three of them were together, but, also, each of them was separate. That dream was late in his analysis, and indicates a resolution of the Oedipal conflicts that he had never had to confront in childhood because his father was successfully obliterated.

Brian

Brian was much more ill than Stephen. Despite his professional success, he was less than half-born, less than half-alive, and drifting towards a state of non-being. Six years of Freudian analysis had freed him of his most distressing symptoms, in particular, a condition of tormenting eczema in his genital area. Though only in his thirties, he had prema-turely aged and resembled an emaciated corpse. Every movement of his body appeared as if premeditated. He said of himself that he was like an automaton going through the motions of living. As a baby he had been unable to suck and had very nearly died of starvation. During his analysis, he frequently remarked he could not take in what I was offering him. In other words, he could not tolerate being fed by me either. Brian had experienced his mother as over-intrusive, and he was never able to look at me, as if he was continuing to stimulate the darkness of the womb. Outside his professional life, Brian was totally passive and unrelated. Clinically, he might have been described as schizoid, although I do not find the labelling of people helpful. This sketchy picture of Brian contains some typical ingredients of half-alive patients; that is, people whose childhood was too disturbed and distorted for all but minimal ego development to have taken place. They are nowhere within sight of the individuation phase that was close to Jung's heart. In the main, they are sexually frozen, often overtly or potentially homosexual, but above all, asexual. This is equally true of both sexes. They go to infinite pains to preserve the semblance of leading "normal" lives, that is, socially acceptable lives, but they only succeed up to a point, more generally in their work. Relentlessly, they go through the motions of appearing tough and independent to cover up the extent of their helplessness and over-dependent attachment to parents. The inevitable crisis occurs when they embark on their first move towards separating.

Brian and I experienced one session when this dilemma had to be lived through and survived by both of us. It followed his cancellation of an appointment with me in favour of a professional engagement with an influential older male client. When he came the next day, he was nearly paralysed and had shrivelled up even further than before. He was unable to speak. Although I was acutely aware of his tormented state, I felt that I should resist the temptation to come to his rescue. To do so might forfeit the possibility of taking him beyond this crisis and assisting him to become alive in his own right. When time was up he hurled his cigarette at me and ran out of my room. He was alight with anger; for the first time I saw in him a nucleus of some life of his own.

This outburst was not like Stephen's rage when his mother focused her attention on the new baby. I have worked with many people who presented as affectively dead and then had a sense of coming to life when they dared to feel emotion.

The following day Brian returned, still very angry, and accused me of failing to understand how suffocated with guilt he had been, having cancelled an appointment with me in favour of a male client. He had opted for the father figure, abandoning me, the mother figure. He was terrified that I would avenge myself by abandoning him. The presence of guilt suggests that a two-person interaction was beginning to develop and that a notion of attack and retaliation, paranoid fears and defensive aggression had been activated. For Brian, up to then, I had almost been the archetypal great mother who had the absolute power of either nurturing or devouring her young. His subsequent comment was significant: "The only thing that can save me now is to rediscover a mother who will breathe life into me". It was then that I understood my reluctance to rescue him. Had I done so, I should have reduced him to a foetus, who has little power to communicate and whose needs are met by primitive, instinctual biological processes.

A passage from Genesis came to mind: "The Lord God formed man of the dust of the ground, and breathed into his nostrils the breath of life, and man became a living soul". Had I yielded to his pressure, I would have turned into an omnipotent goddess for him. Had I become a numinous archetypal figure, I would have lost for Brian my fallible human qualities, the very attributes that assist in mediating archetypal forces. By renouncing that role, I had steered him into some contact with the fragment of the father within him and whatever atrophied masculinity he possessed. As he left, he looked me in the eye for the first time. The point of dissolution of the illusion of "oneness" had arrived.

Whenever he perceived himself as other than an extension of his parents' personalities and as straying from their rigid image of him Brian was overcome by guilt. His father had wanted his only son to be tough, extroverted, and successful, a near-impossible target for such a frail, introverted person as Brian, although to some degree he had met his father's expectations in his work situation. In Brian's words: "To be myself was unacceptable to my father. My mother, on the other hand, wanted me to be her perfect image of a son, so that I should make her feel a perfect mother. She fascinates and repels me simultaneously, and I feel terrible because I don't love her in the way she wants me to. I cannot risk revealing myself to her. I possess no personality in relation to her. I have betrayed my mother and need to protect her from realizing it. I am not what she thinks. If I were to rebel, the world would come to an end—my parents would be destroyed. I would do irreparable harm."

Searles (1961) speaks of patients whose existence as children in their own right received little acknowledgement, i.e., they existed mainly as an extension of their parents' personalities. Searles argues that this may lead to a conviction in the patient that he "possesses some magical, inhumanly destructive power over people". Brian could not allow himself to have any manifest, discernible sexual life of his own that involved *another* person. To do so would have disproved the fact that he was still part of his mother's body, and establish instead that he owned his body in his own right. His marriage of many years remained unconsummated. His sexual life, such as it was, was enacted in the secret dark recesses of his bachelor bedroom, where he masturbated by stimulating himself with sadistic photographs in which women were being beaten and subjugated. In this situation he could feel that he was top dog. It excited him. In addition, he indulged in weekly feasts alone, going to expensive restaurants and indulging in large amounts of food and drink. From there, he would take himself to a sleazy pornographic club where women publicly humiliated themselves. Furtively, he went home to masturbate. These pursuits constituted the only pleasure in his life and the only stronghold against complete engulfment by his mother. If they had been interfered with, his frustrated, murderous impulses would have threatened to overwhelm and disintegrate him. He would have become even more paralysed. Open rebellion would have killed his mother. To preserve her, he could at best afford to be less than half-alive.

I should like to say something about the problem of inhibited aggression in the analysis of patients such as Brian. I trust that I have given enough material to demonstrate that even a show of forcefulness strikes them as an uncontrollable explosion, which threatens the shattering of everything and of everyone. Instead, the analyst is commonly confronted by passive withdrawal, or by a withdrawn paranoid response. Rage is turned inwards, producing depression, if not despair, to avoid the obliteration of the indispensable other. The venting of aggression against the seemingly indispensable "mother" figure is too hazardous, unless the father, the masculine component, can be experienced as protecting and preserving her from the wounds of attack and ultimate separation. Up to this point, I have been focusing on a father seen as weak, dismissible, and overshadowed by the mother.

My last two clinical examples briefly illustrate a father experienced as "absent" in the sense that he was violent, drunk, unpredictable, unrelated and unloving, eventually removed from the family with the active assistance of the patient when a child. Thus, these patients were deprived of nurturing experience from both parents. (Both mothers were emotionally unrelated not only to their husbands but to their children too.)

Sheila

Sheila had a barren childhood; she was a lonely, manipulating, depressed woman, who threatened suicide whenever she felt the illusory "union" that she imagined she had with me was at risk. I was the first and only person to whom she felt close; I regard her now as the most difficult and alarming patient with whom I have worked. She had never experienced love from either parent, nor did any affection exist between her parents. They were divorced when she was in her early teens. As far as I was concerned, she had a "delusional transference"—she was besotted with me. The most infinitessimal change would upset her out of all proportion. Inwardly, she would scream desperately, like a young baby disrupted at the breast. When I moved house, she was in a severe crisis, as if her small, familiar world had totally disintegrated. After saying that she had lost me, she pronounced that she too was going away. Although I was deeply affected, and feared that she was going away to die, I felt that I must let her go, despite my own, as well as her, investment in her analysis. The following day, to my everlasting relief, she screamed over the telephone at me that if she had ended her life, she would also have lost me, like throwing out the baby with the bath water. Therefore, she would return for her sessions.

Her background and Tom's were not dissimilar. Both of them described their mothers as withdrawn, depressed and martyred, and their fathers as violent, destructive, with terrifying outbursts of rage. They were feeling, as they both did, that they were in the grip of a more formidable archetypal partner, namely the great mother, in her idealized and in her devouring aspects. The clinical picture of half-aliveness is even more entrenched if there is an "absent" mother, who cannot at all mediate some experience of humanity, love, and holding; the damage far outweighs that inflicted by the suffocating, over-possessive mothers of Stephen or Brian. These people live in an emotional desert, as did their parents, and consequently they manifest schizoid traits and an overwhelming longing to be reincorporated inside the mother–analyst, which they see as their only secure experience. Whenever Sheila could not avoid the realization that she did not posses me utterly, she attacked me venomously and unmercifully. Gradually, I was able to tolerate her onslaughts better. This occurred when I managed to constellate within myself both my feminine and masculine aspects; that is, I united my own internalized mother and father. In other words, whenever Sheila succeeded in splitting the parents within me, thus separating me from my animus, I became part of her chaos, and I would take evasive action, which only heightened her destructiveness and guilt. Her ego boundaries were as fragile as a young infant's might be at 6–9 months, in the grip of both love and hatred, i.e., at the onset of the "depressive position". They needed shoring up in the form of a mother–father unity before she was safe enough to express both her positive and her negative feelings. During one crisis she actually said: "I need the father in you too." She only came close to achieving an integrated emotional state when she received in her analysis the psychological experience of two united, loving parents. It was at such times that a benevolent regression could take place; she would speak of her longing to be my baby inside me. Only as a foetus, she maintained, had she ever felt safe, wanted, and cherished.

Sheila claimed that her parents used to tear each other to pieces. She became a pawn; they tried to win her over to one side or the other. The culmination of these conflicts occurred when she was forced to give evidence in a divorce court. Knowingly, she lied about her father, so that her mother might win the case. From that time on, she disintegrated rapidly, the more so because her worst fear, that she had caused the split between her parents, was confirmed by reality, demolishing any surviving phantasy of a loving pair. At one point, when I had become excessively concerned about her suicidal threats. I arranged for her to see a male psychiatric colleague. She came away with a sense that both he and I cared about her and that she could safely share *both* mother *and* father without depriving either of them. The outcome was a spontaneous alleviation of a near-psychotic depression; she felt wanted and a shared object of concern.

Her parents' failure to come to terms with one another was matched by their incapacity to relate to Sheila as a whole person. That had produced a far-reaching rupture in her personality. She had no experience of wholeness either outside or within herself; she described herself as "torn to pieces", or "all in bits". I had observed that she, like Tom, was quite incapable of retaining the memory of one session to the next, even when her sessions were on consecutive days. Experiences of fragmentation can occur irrespective of the parental situation; these states are indicative of a fragile ego being overwhelmed by archetypal forces. In another instance, a patient who was becoming better integrated and fulfilled convinced herself that her newly acquired strength had been stolen from her husband. She felt that she had irrevocably wounded him, and a period of guilt and hopelessness ensued.

Tom

Tom began his analysis by rigidly denying his dependency needs. In his sessions, he was so controlling that I was totally blotted out and blocked. He spoke compulsively into empty space, an attempt, as I saw it, to hold me to him inextricably. I felt as isolated and useless as he. Then one day, when, as usual, he was flooding me with words, I said quietly: "You know, you don't *have* to." The effect was dramatic. For the first time, he relaxed; then added that the only excitement in his life was derived from observing pretty young women at a distance. He had always avoided looking at me because, he said, if he were to become aware of me as a separate entity, his much-needed phantasy of "oneness" with me would become disturbed. He could not permit me to show him in or out of my consulting-room, as was my custom; that would have exposed the fact that there were two of us. It was *he* who terminated each session. Whenever a holiday break approached he pleaded for extra sessions so that the ritual number of sessions, which represented his regular feeds and safety to him, should be maintained. In a letter written during the first year of his analysis, he included the following: "It is almost as if I am a prisoner in a cell. The door is ajar, yet I dare not go out into the bright world. I remain fixed where I am— rigid, terror-stricken, immovable. My present non-existence, in a contrary way, is burning me out . . . so much of my energy goes into suppressing and stifling my individuality and spontaneity."

Conclusion

My work with patients such as Stephen, Brian, Sheila, and Tom has shown that an integral, vital stage in the healing process necessitates a reactivation in the patient's unconscious of a steadfast mother–father constellation. Only thus does it become endurable for the patient to relinquish the primary, phantasized state of "union" with his actual, or with the archetypal, mother. The inhibiting effect of divided parents on growth and development can be devastating. Should the analysis go well, however, that area of the patient's personality that has been committed to a real or imaginary "oneness" with the mother, and was thus unavailable for the enrichment of his own life, will gradually be restored to him, making him more alive, more whole. With the re-emergence of the father as an important person, the mother can gradually be safely relinquished by him, and she is no longer perceived as mutilated and impoverished. Briefly, I see the process of reconciling the parents within as a vital ingredient in healing.

Summary

This chapter is the outcome of observations made through my analytic work as well as the more than twenty years spent doing marital therapy at the Tavistock Institute of Marital Studies. Although primarily concerned with the inner world, I acknowledge the frequent tragic and damaging impact that the escalating divorce rates have on children who consequently grow up in "one-parent" families. Clinical material and a diagram are presented to illustrate my contention that "half-aliveness" is often linked with an emotionally "absent" parent, in my cases more frequently the father. Furthermore, it follows that there is an "absent" husband also, so that the parental marriage tends to be dilapidated and empty to a degree that lumbers the unfortunate child, most likely the only son, with the role of the surrogate "husband", a psychological trap from which he may be unable to extricate himself well into adult life. It is suggested that a resolution to this pathological enmeshment may lead to a symbolic, if not actual, reinstatement of the "absent" parent, enabling a reconciliation of the inner parents to take place, which then frees the previously "paralysed" individual to discover his own identity, liberating his hitherto atrophied resources.

* * *

Tom's pictures

I can well afford to be brief as his paintings speak for themselves. The first (Figure 2) was done in the early phase of his analysis and is quite devastating in its portrayal of his psychic and physical torment. The second (Figure 3), done about two years on, is much more benign. The atom bomb explodes far behind him in the distance and Tom is waving safely with his head above the water in the company of the fish. The colours are peaceful compared to his first picture.

Figure 2.

Figure 3.

CHAPTER THREE

A psychological study of anorexia nervosa: an account of the relationship between psychic factors and bodily functioning

P sychosomatic illness constitutes a cry of despair and of hope, and may represent an unsuccessful attempt at a search for wholeness. It points to a division within the individual, and any therapeutic confrontation needs therefore to attempt to encompass all aspects of the patient. When a psychosomatic disorder such as a severe eating disturbance manifests itself and could threaten the continuance of life, the pressure on the analyst to focus primarily on the symptom may become difficult to resist.

A scanning of current psychiatric literature on anorexia nervosa is a Herculean task. *Psychiatric Briefs*, 8(1) (1975) alone contains eleven extracts from the most recent publications on this topic. In the present cultural environment, and at a point in time when sylph-like slimness is at a premium, eating disorders foist themselves as a socially acceptable manifestation on to the disturbed psyche of the individual. Furthermore, the very real danger to health, and, indeed, to survival, together with the acute distress that these patients cause their relatives and medical practitioners, is matched by their resourceful guile and cunning in sabotaging traditional medical and psychiatric measures. Their scheming to resist a "cure" is equal to that of alcoholics. Though "behavioural" and "conditioning" techniques are widely favoured because, ostensibly, they produce a considerable percentage of "successful cures", I am inclined to suspend judgement on their long-term efficacy and retain the view that it may be futile to aim only at a cure of the physical condition that masks a fragmented, stunted personality. As Jung and others have shown us, a heart ailment, for instance, need not arise from the heart only; it can also arise from the psyche of the sufferer, and then its resolution may evolve from symbolic growth; that is, a gradual inner transformation. Meier (1963) concludes that healing can take place only through the constellation of a symbol, or the archetype of totality.

My own interest in eating disorders was triggered off when I found myself working simultaneously with four patients whose ostensible central preoccupation was with food. Their lives were taken over by incessant compulsive eating rituals of alternate starving and gorging, often followed by vomiting. They went through either acute phases of elation, or feelings of guilt and worthlessness, and I need hardly add that all four were alarmingly underweight or overweight at times. I will now quote you a standard psychiatric textbook description of anorexia nervosa.

> Anorexia nervosa occurs typically in girls in their later teens and in young unmarried women; it is doubtful if the same syndrome is found in men. A typical triad of symptoms is anorexia, amenorrhoea and loss of weight. Vomiting is common, representing repressed disgust; it is rapid and easy, occurring without nausea. The illness has an emotional basis. These girls tend to come from families with a history of nutritional disturbances, obesity and anorexia. There is a refusal to take an adequate diet, or phases of compulsive overeating countered by vomiting and excessive purgation. A remarkable feature is tireless activity in spite of emaciation. The patient may declare that she is perfectly alright. She may exhibit the belle indifference of the hysteric. Depression may be prominent, with feelings of guilt and isolation and suicidal thoughts. Obsessional, anxious and hypochondriacal traits are encountered. There are food fads and alimentary preoccupations. There may be a severely disturbed mother/daughter relationship, the patient being at one and the same time unduly dependent and rebelling against maternal domination. The prognosis is poor; only 10–20 percent recover. [Henderson & Gillespie, 1969]

What heightened my interest was the fact that only one of my four patients appeared to fit the above description closely, though even here not only the mother but the father too entered significantly into the constellation of her illness. This, my first case, concerns Alice, a young unmarried woman in her early twenties. I had known her parents on and off for approximately five years in connection with marital problems. The mother was as thin as a beanstalk, had many physical illnesses, and was remote and detached. She gave the impression that she felt in some strange way triumphant about her husband's marital and sexual deviations. On the other hand, she had an unusually close relationship with Alice. For instance, they used to bathe together and to scrub each other's backs. The intimate marriage seemed to be between mother and daughter and not between the parents. Not surprisingly, it was Alice's father who contacted me on this occasion, whereas before he had come only reluctantly and under duress from his wife. He told me that Alice had recently returned from her first stay away from home, depressed, ill, and with severe eating difficulties. She had lost four stone in weight and her periods had stopped.

Hilde Bruch, in her book *Eating Disorders and the Person Within* (1974), stresses the importance of involving the family in the treatment process. She further points out that whatever the anorexia patient does is not for herself but for her parents' sake, though it can never be sufficient to please them. It frequently happens that the patient's mother is dissatisfied with her marriage and endows the child with the task of compensating for her own disappointment. Thus, she suffocates her daughter's pull towards independence. Both parents conceal their deep disillusionment with each other. Secretly, they carry on a sacrificial competition. Each desires the sympathy and support of the child, whose energies go towards satisfying the competitive claims of the parents so that too little is left over for investment in her own development. The quote below emphasizes these points:

> It appears that ultimate progress for the patient is importantly related to the initial levels of psychoneurotic status of the parents. The overall findings in the study support the view that anorexia nervosa is often importantly and dynamically related to parental and family psychoneurotic morbidity and stress the importance of

investigating the illness in terms of the family pathology and the probable related importance of involving parents in the treatment programme. [Crisp, Harding, & McGuinness, 1974]

To return to Alice: when her father suggested that he and his wife should come and discuss their daughter's illness with me, I thought this device of excluding Alice might prejudice any prospect of my working with her and her parents in the future, and so I proposed that all three come together. From previous contact with them, I had a hunch that a conjoint technique might be the most appropriate. I knew this approach had been used successfully by many other therapists in the past, as this extract suggests:

> The marital relationship was inadequate, allowing J. to be inappropriately involved in the parents' affairs. The family's pattern of functioning was characterized by over-protectiveness, lack of privacy for individual members, denial of the existence of any problems other than J.'s illness, and a failure to resolve marital conflicts which remained concealed by the parents' preoccupation with J. Her symptoms were therefore reinforced within the family circle. [Liebman, Minuchin, & Baker, 1974]

Alice looked like a Giacometti sculpture: emaciated, withdrawn, and distraught. Her father was noticeably depressed and agitated, as if in some way he felt to blame and implicated. Her mother once again seemed least affected, almost as if exulting in the catastrophic manner in which Alice had returned to the fold. Alice and her father did most of the talking, haltingly. The dominant theme was Alice's acute guilt and agitation about having left her mother in pursuit of a life of her own. Father seemed only too well aware of his neglect of his wife, and how he had handed over responsibility for her to Alice.

I explained that guilt tends to produce illness with the unconscious purpose of restoring the status quo. In the process, inevitably someone is made to suffer. I pointed out to them how the family problems were being passed around between them like a parcel. As usual, the weakest link in the chain, Alice, had become lumbered with the parcel, not daring to unwrap it or to pass it on. She had become the casualty, while her father, in spite of his depression and feelings of blame, was still able to keep up appearances and to function in the world.

Towards the end of the interview the mother mentioned casually that, at their request, their family doctor had referred Alice to a Psychiatric

Outpatients' Department. Why, then, I asked myself, had they come to see me at all? In retrospect, I think it was to find absolution, and not a resolution. I could not, because of the arrangements they had committed themselves to, continue with them, and this I told them. The unconscious conspiracy to treat the symptom and to neglect the person within had won the day and sabotaged a potentially favourable prognosis engendered by this first family session.

Within a week, and before she had been seen at the Outpatients' Department, Alice's mother sent me a letter from which I quote: "Alice is looking better; some of the strain is leaving her face and she is eating more normally. Her weight is increasing. I feel she is being repaired". Some nine months later, however, I heard from mother again. Alice had had a course of electro-convulsion therapy and was on anti-depressants and tranquillizers. Mother and father were also being treated with drugs. Alice had regained some weight but was still depressed and not menstruating, nor able to function in any facet of her life.

She was continually asking, "When will I be allowed to talk to someone?"

This brief and frustrating encounter with Alice has had a happier sequence. She subsequently telephoned me out of her own motivation, asking for therapy. Just two years after our first meeting I have seen her once and plan to take her on regularly.

I was struck by her frail beauty. She looked like a fairy-tale princess, waiting for her prince to awaken her, and as if made of fragile, precious china.

Alice told me that she had become dissatisfied with her treatment, was still on drugs and receiving five minutes' follow-up therapy fortnightly at the Outpatient Department. She felt annoyed when told that her parents were narrow-minded Christians, and that she should take herself off and have sex. Her weight, however, has stabilized at 114 lbs under the threat of hospitalization if it falls below 112 lbs. Her parents have meanwhile moved to another city and have set her up in an apartment in the house of an elderly couple who stand in for them. Alice is lonely, having no friends of her own age, is doing a rather low-grade job well below her capacity, and is still depressed and feels too fat.

At this point I should like to quote an extract from another article on this topic, entitled "Mind over matter":

The more accessible material suggested that all dimensions of psychic life were experienced in terms of the quantity of their flesh and the oral activities directly related thereto. All described a deliberate decision not to eat based on the dual concept that they were too fat and that eating was bad. Their attitude towards feeding others was much more accepting. . . . The patients were encouraged to lose the fear of pleasure from which many of them clearly suffered. [Galdston, 1974]

Alice has bouts of stealing food from the couple that she lived with, and has carbohydrate binges, stuffing herself with "forbidden" food. On the other hand, she has difficulties about eating in company, was afraid she may be pressed to eat starch—yet steals it. She was also afraid of being cheated of her due, of being denied that to which she feels entitled, and is touchy about being offered a smaller helping or else forgotten altogether. These contradictions pinpoint my view that food is a stand-in for love and caring. Alice also finds herself acutely critical of what other people eat, a manifestation of her resentment of her parents.

She felt "unattractive and babyish", obsessed with and anxious about feeling left out and not being given enough. Her mother, who was a poor housekeeper and cook, encouraged Alice to spend her weekends with her parents, preparing their meals for them. Yet Alice felt her parents were "not really there" and, most of all, not there for her, being still very entangled with her mother, whom she sees as lonely and not appreciated, although father had told her "mother is stronger than you think". In spite of struggling to distance herself from her parents, their mutual entanglement is still very strong; Alice sees herself as the only one who really understands how her mother feels.

Alice avoids involvement with other people, ostensibly because she would then have to eat with them. If, nevertheless, she becomes attracted to a man or makes a "conquest", she persuades herself that she has become "bored" with him. Her acquaintances are married couples, and she befriends the husband on an intellectual level, which she feels is "safe". At twenty-five, she continues to feel that no one takes her seriously, or cares enough to show true concern either for herself or for her mother. Whenever she allows herself to think about all of this, she gets profoundly upset on behalf of the mother in her, and of her baby self.

I recently came across an article in the *American Journal of Psychiatry* on the effectiveness of "Family therapy in the treatment of anorexia nervosa" (Barcal, 1971). The author's experiences accentuate my own. Thus, he describes how the anorexia families he has worked with manifest concern and interest for one another while denying personal wishes and interests. Family members had to guess in order to determine the other's wishes; a direct expression of need was taboo, thus creating flux states of involvement together with abandonment. Their bodies were strange and alien to them. He further stresses that the families were living under an umbrella of falsehood; a person who is unable to differentiate between hunger and other needs becomes anorexic as a perverse way of solving conflicts. He points out the necessity for "peace at all costs", engendering guilt and an abdication of responsibility, isolation and a power struggle for control. The aim of his therapy was to enable the patient to take over the responsibility for herself, and to neutralize the eating symptoms. If successful, an inadvertent and alarming reaction tended to occur in the other family members, as was the case with Alice, whose parents were not only an important component of her illness, but subsequently became so disturbed that they too received drug therapy at the Psychiatric Outpatient Department where Alice was being treated.

In a paper entitled "Hungry patients: reflections on ego structure", Plaut (1959) outlines the basic problems of patients who were predominantly occupied with food and eating. The following quote summarizes the gist of his article:

> Somatic symptoms have a psychic basis. Hungry patients have not yet acquired the capacity to relate to whole persons or images, but only to parts. There is an absence of ego boundaries, i.e. a stage of magical identity in which there is no distinction between you and I. The aim is to unify the ego sufficiently to distinguish between itself and the other, between an inner and an outer world. Experiences of wholeness remain exclusively linked with the object which stands proxy for the patient's own ego. Bodily experiences in infancy have not been satisfying. [Plaut, 1959]

Personally, I should go even further, and describe my own patients as more than hungry; they are craving not for food but for love. The state of magical identity referred to above appears to have become one of primary identity; i.e., anorexia patients try to achieve an imaginary state of bliss and contentment associated with the original fusion between subject and object, between baby and mother. This illusory primary object is the ever-nourishing breast—they are obsessed with it. The exclusive, inexhaustible supplier of nourishment comes closest to how they would like to perceive themselves. This identification temporarily enhances their tenuous self-esteem and promises the approval of others. It gives them a sense of power and achievement. To maintain it, however, they must ensure that they are in absolute control as the sole manipulator of all nourishment dispensed, withheld, or rejected. Thereby, their mother is divested of other positive feeding, loving qualities; she is, as it were, dethroned, if not mutilated. This engenders acute guilt in the patients, and fears of mother's hatred and revenge. Thus, the idealized breast has been transformed into the terrible one, and the powerful, manipulating patient sees herself as the perpetrator of the deed. This complex cycle leads to an intolerable psychological trap in which the patient revolves from a temporary state of bliss and effectiveness to becoming a depleted and greedy monster. In fact, both the subject and the object have turned into monstrous breast-witches, and the identification is so complete that it cannot be disentangled.

At this point, we have moved closer to some understanding of why these particular patients appear to become fixated at the primary oral level rather than develop other forms of neuroses. In all my four anorexia cases, the patient's actual mother is seen as precisely fitting the fantasy monster–breast just described. There is an uncanny correspondence between the internal fantasy and the external reality, the one reinforcing the other. Their mutual stranglehold takes on archetypal proportions, not mediated by redeeming personal experiences.

One way out for patients in these situations is to retreat into a state resembling an intra-uterine, conflict-free shelter, a depressed withdrawal. There are two alternatives—to starve until they almost disappear, or to seek relief in an eating binge in which they once again get on to the bandwagon, creating for themselves an illusory ever-full breast. But then their excessive greed evokes revulsion, anxiety, and shame, and the vomiting mechanism usually becomes active at this point. The whole syndrome is cyclical and continuous. Indeed, I have observed that those of my anorexic patients who have children of their own perpetuate this pattern in the next generation, both over-indulging and excessively controlling them, while plagued by fantasies of ridding themselves of them for good and all.

I am quite convinced that inadequate and unsympathetic mothering experiences set the stage for the subsequent pathology of anorexia. Wilke (1971) also stresses the predominance of the mother-complex and any immaturity of personality in heart neurotics. In the same way, anorexia patients have never been able really to depend on anyone, and even in infancy lacked the experience of a need being adequately met. Thus, they fail to differentiate other signals of discomfort from pangs of hunger, and food provides a temporary relief, whatever the source of deprivation or anxiety. Severe love bereavement leads to mistrust of the legitimacy of all other feelings and ultimately has an annihilating effect. There is, therefore, a desire to become larger and larger, or else to disappear and, perhaps, to have a new beginning, a rebirth.

Other psychosomatic disorders and psychosexual problems frequently accompany anorexia. In any encounter with the opposite sex, for instance, an overpowering craving for affection clashes with fear and revulsion. During an erotic act, their fragile sense of personal ego consciousness disappears, sweeping with it the last vestige of an identity of their own. The encroachment of the partner's ego is intolerable, yet longed for.

Two of my four patients suffered from migraine and attacks of dizziness, which I understood as a shrinking from a longed-for, yet feared, sensation of autonomy. The connection between asthma and migraine makes good sense in this context. These symptoms exemplify opposites—the fear of the suffocating mother and the complementary dread of separateness from her. One of my migraine patients had an asthmatic child. Kierkegaard's (1983) words spring to mind: "Freedom looks down into its own possibilities, and then grasps desperately for limitations in an attempt to survive". The basic task for the analyst with anorexia patients, as I see it, is to focus on their real needs, and not to focus on the illness. Any attempt to persuade the patient to eat or not to eat should be avoided; the underlying disturbances, however, have to be brought into the open whenever possible. Any dwelling on vomiting or other somatic symptoms only leads to a neglect of vital but hidden aspects. As suggested earlier, the analyst will try to find a way to stand proxy for the missing ego in lieu of the person with whom the patient is identified. As the ego boundaries grow stronger and more flexible, interpretations become increasingly possible and certainly necessary. The emphasis needs to be on the implicit regression to earlier levels and on a reconstruction of them. In the main, however, therapy with these patients consists in listening to them, an experience they have missed out on. The therapist who presumes to know the answer plays into his patient's belief that somebody else has the magical solution in the same way that mother purported to have.

My next case is an example of the atypical within the familiar.

Barbara displayed the usual somatic manifestation of anorexia. In fact, after two previous analyses she had become, and was determined to remain, a chronic case. She was already in her fifties but looked even older and haggard; she was married and had had children. In addition to her eating problems, she demonstrated another characteristic feature of anorexia: the pathological envy of whoever is perceived as the best loved within the family setting—most often it is the sibling of the other sex. In her case, these acute feelings of envy culminated in murderous attacks on the one she perceived as her parents' favourite son, or else in futile attempts to become like him, and even to surpass him.

A negative prognosis was determined from the start, when she insisted she could only come once a week. It was clear to both of us that her resistance to change was paramount; all my interpretations on this point were stonewalled by her. Nevertheless, because of the empathy between us, I became a perfect foil for her anorexia nervosa mechanisms. Whenever something incisive had taken place in a session, she vomited it out in the form of a meaningful but almost illegible scrawl that she posted to me, telling me in substance that she had been fed too much, so that it had turned bad inside her, and she would starve herself by not coming next time. In this self-defeating manner she wasted my time and her money, while remaining craving and desperate. The only time that she felt any good was when she could produce a dream. However innocuous the dream might be, it provided her with a sliver of confirmation that she possessed some inner life that was her own.

In an early session she drew my attention to an arrangement of wild flowers in my room. She disapproved of my liking for "rubbish", as she called it. She also seemingly disapproved of my liking of her. The next day she wrote as follows: "I was offended when you told me in connection with these weeds that everything, however apparently valueless, can be accepted and treated as something that has meaning. I want so much from you, yet I get nothing. Good things in excess turn bad". Not surprisingly, she was a compulsive, self-induced vomiter.

A few sessions later she wrote: "Loving feelings are dangerous and obliterate boundaries. They make one take other people inside one's self and get mixed up with them, and one has to get rid of them, suddenly, violently. I have to spoil things to protect them from the murderous feelings inside me. Then I become an empty shell without life. I don't know where I begin and end. I am drained and impaired. Her one relief was strenuous and endless walking to the point of exhaustion.

Her mother was seen by her as dominant and insecure, narcissistic, a "Virgin Queen", and childish. Mother had food fads and starved herself on a nature cure diet. Father was seen as only interested in mother, and never stood up for Barbara. Mother constantly criticized Barbara, calling her greedy, fat, ugly, awkward, stupid, and frequently pointed out to her that her mouth was permanently open, and that she was ashamed of her. Barbara had had thirteen governesses in twelve years! She further described her mother as a "jealous prima donna" who never accepted any "nice" feelings from her. She remembered an occasion when she borrowed her mother's bicycle without permission and slightly damaged it. Her mother rejected her plea to be allowed to repair it, and instead pulled Barbara all the way home by her hair.

Barbara's eating habits followed the characteristic pattern: she ate too much of the "good" things and vomited, or she starved herself, or she ate the "wrong" food. "Greed takes over," she said, "and I feel ugly." She also had the typical distorted body image which I hope shows in the little primitive self-portrait she drew (Figure 1). It shows a scare-crow-like person with a tiny pinched-in waist, two minute appendages instead of legs, no hands, but greatly magnified buttocks. Behind this figure it is just possible to detect another, a portrait outline of a timid-looking young girl. I felt this depicted her undeveloped young self.

Barbara did not know how to use her hands, and was prone to say that it was as if she had none. She explained "words are better"; she read greedily, but could never retain any of it.

When I interpreted to her that she dared not use her hands because of other murderous impulses engendered by her envy, she remembered confirmatory data. She had tried her utmost to be a tomboy—a tougher and better boy than her brother. On one occasion in her teens when her

Figure 1.

brother taunted her with being "jelly-muscled", she throttled him until he was blue in the face, and then bashed him so hard that she broke his nose.

Barbara left me abruptly when a distressing event occurred in her life, and when she could have done with maximal support. She bequeathed an unpaid bill as the surviving bond between us.

Munch's "The Scream" (Figure 2) haunted me while I was gestating this chapter. I feel it projects cogently the agony of the anorexia nervosa patient confronted by the monster within and without, and catches the expression I have often seen in the faces of these patients.

Both Eileen and Douglas, my third and fourth cases, have now moved in the direction of integration. They have had long analyses with frequent sessions, though, interestingly, their anorexia symptomatology only became prominent in certain phases of their therapy.

Eileen, like Barbara, was atypical in that she was married with children, and she was menstruating regularly, though with much accompanying disturbance. Her relentless pursuit of thinness is a recent development, and follows many years of frequent and acute attacks of migraine, severe phobic states, and hypochondriacal preoccupations, as well as compulsive over-eating with obesity and numerous psychosexual difficulties. She was obese when she first came to see me, and subsequently

Figure 2.

did a complete turn-about. I shall be confining my comments to her starvation phase, from which she was in the process of emerging.

She was the daughter of a suffering mother, who was said to have conceived Eileen in her sleep, and who sobbed her heart out when she gave birth to a girl; to be female was a catastrophe! It meant a life of misery. Eileen had to be her mother's perpetual "sunshine", so had never really been a child; she never played, was always called "Sunshine", and never heard her own name. If she behaved like a small child, mother would become ill and suffer. She was smothered by her mother. Everything that happened was said to be Eileen's fault. She felt compelled to be what her mother needed of her and felt incessantly watched, assessed, and judged. To be unhappy would have implied an insult to her mother's supposed superiority. Thus, Eileen acquired the façade of adequate functioning and learned to mistrust the legitimacy of all her own feelings, suffering severe love deprivation, for which she attempted to compensate by a promiscuous phase in adolescence that revolted her and made her ashamed. Unable to live a life of her own, she lived by proxy through other people.

I quote a relevant extract from a recent publication:

From the psychodynamic point of view, the reduction in food consumption is an expression of an unconscious revolt of the anorexic patient against her own body. The condition is associated with an abnormal affective relation between mother and daughter; the former is excessively anxious and concerned about the well-being of the latter, who feels that her growing body frustrates her unconscious desire to remain a child. [Rolandi, Azzolini, & Barabino, 1973]

As already described, a sense of hollowness within can be temporarily ameliorated by filling up with food; the eating stands in for satisfaction of needs in other areas, and provides a momentary sense of spurious power. With Eileen, elation, however, did not last, and she would soon say that she wanted to disappear, or at least to have a boy's figure like her brother so as to be admired. She would then make herself vomit by putting her finger down her throat. Her eating habits became so highly ritualized and followed such a precise sequence that they acted as an anaesthetic. She was weighing herself several times a day, and each fresh loss of weight gave her a sense of triumph; it was a "bonus" which made her feel superior because it proved her powers of self-control, but it was never good enough, and she set herself a yet lower target than before.

Her distorted body image, which, like Barbara's, was of bizarre proportions, was, however, gradually becoming more realistic, and her anorexic symptoms were beginning to phase themselves out. To achieve this she had to go back and begin again as a baby with a different mother figure—that is, myself.

The aim of the first phase of therapy is to continue the role of the mother with the exclusion of the negative aspects. "Transference" can be achieved only by attempts to break through the voluntary self-isolation of the patient. [Schenck & Deegener, 1974]

In fact, when Eileen made insistent demands on me to be treated as a baby, I felt the vital turning point towards health had begun. Even so she still felt too large, all bulk without appeal, useless, with ugly hands, neither in nor out of the womb. "I am a stone walking about, a stone feels nothing." She would avert her eyes, looking without seeing, and imagining, like a baby playing hide and seek, that she would not be seen either. Nevertheless, her face that she has hated has become less fixed and staring, her mouth less pouting and sulking, and she has learned to smile as well as to become very sad, because she has relinquished her exclusive living through others. She has become alive and rebellious:

"Why should I do what is expected? As long as I have a beginning I can persevere. It's my turn now; it has never been my turn. I have been crippled, and feel the pain of a crippled child. When I am I, you can be you! I am detaching myself inside myself. I want my own face, which I don't know yet. I am growing up, and am experiencing and beginning to like my body. I want to be me now."

Gradually, she started crying from her guts; for years she had shed invisible tears. She explained: "When I howl there is so much inside me. I feel myself getting smaller and smaller, three years old, and then only four weeks old, and then I begin to exist as me." Now she often eats normally, no longer having to starve or to gorge herself constantly, and to make herself sick, and no longer feels constantly watched, assessed, and judged. She is finding herself and how to be alone without a sense of intolerable rejection.

My last case, Douglas, is also atypical in being a man, and in his sixties.

Douglas has come perilously close to death on several occasions—accidents in which he seems to have had to test out his own resources for survival to the ultimate point. He is still alarmingly emaciated, and he used to sprawl on the chair as if he had no body structure at all. He had been totally controlled by his mother, the more so after his father had died when Douglas was only three. Recently it has become noticeable that Douglas sits up tall and becomes more of a person when an interpretation goes home and reaches his core. Latterly, he has had two crucial dreams. In one he shouted, "I have had enough of interfering women!" He then "forgot" to come for his subsequent session, in spite of his over-meticulous timekeeping. His dependence–rebellion conflict in relation to me as his mother had become too much for him. Shortly afterwards he had a dream in which his mother's hands were round his neck, and she had a stranglehold on him from behind. He bit her and shouted, "Let go of me!"

Attacks of uncontrollable vomiting have recently occurred only when he goes out for a meal and eats in public; then he again feels dependent and controlled, or guilty and anxious because of his greed and extravagance, or else overcome by his frustration and rage because the food or the service have not come up to scratch. Attacks of migraine and dizziness, frequent at one time, have become spasmodic. They have always been linked with his having it too good, some achievement or success for himself, which was not of immediate benefit to his current mother figure, or with an increasing sense of new-won freedom, which frightened him. He is now almost ready to terminate his analysis, but scared to death of an ending, which, in his case, actually coincides with the afternoon of his life.

I will now summarize my main points. I had originally called the paper that has become this chapter "Metamorphosis in reverse", because the transition, which one hopes will take place, is not from the simple to the complex, as in nature, but from the multi-faceted, ostensibly somatic syndrome to its basic, primary, emotional constituents in infancy.

With anorexic patients a distorted attitude towards, and an abnormal preoccupation with, food is central to their lives and constitutes a regression and fixation to an early oral level of development. The nutritional function is used in an attempt to solve or camouflage complex emotional and interpersonal problems.

The triggering-off point for the subsequent syndrome appears to be the mother's inappropriate response to her infant's needs from birth into adulthood, and one must hypothesize that unsatisfying feeding experiences occur together with continuing distortions of communications on other levels. These factors lead to a stunting or deformation of the ego structure, a distorted body concept and arrested psychological growth. Because of these defects, the patient's eating disorder constitutes a futile attempt to be in control of his own life. The symptoms constitute a pathological attempt at acquiring some identity and trying to fulfil the insatiable craving for seemingly unobtainable love.

I have drawn attention to the uncanny degree of correspondence between the subject and the object, i.e., between a patient's fantasy image of herself as a powerful menacing breast–monster and her experience and perception of her actual mother. A mutual strangle-hold situation results in which both the child and the mother reject each other while being indispensable to one another, thus engendering murderous feelings in both. The fathers in all my cases did not intervene or rescue the child. Sibling rivalry is more than usually acute, the sibling of the opposite sex always being perceived as the favourite child, and the patient unsuccessfully endeavouring to demolish the rival, to surpass him, or to turn into him by changing shape.

Psychosexual disturbances, other psychosomatic symptoms, and a preoccupation with death as well as the longing for a new start are encountered. The anorexia patient attempts to become omnipotent and indestructible by over-eating, or else tries to do away with herself by starvation and shrinkage, in the hope of resurrection as the best loved. If therapy fails, she will eventually die, but it is to be hoped that she will survive and evolve towards experiencing herself as a person to be cherished.

* * *

Postscript
I have had Christmas cards from Alice, who is now happily married with children.

CHAPTER FOUR

Relationships and the growth of personality

Co-written with colleagues at the Family Discussion Bureau

T he love relationship of man and woman that builds itself into a marital union invites more of our interest and empathy than any other human relationship except, perhaps, that of parent and child. The seeking for this adult relationship, its preservation and its development towards parenthood, are among the deepest aspirations of almost everyone. Its rights and its duties are jealously guarded by the individual. The high evaluation of its importance for the individual is endorsed by far-reaching social measures and many institutions. The unravelling and reknitting of the complex strands that make up this intimate relationship, its conflicts and satisfactions, is the concern of this introduction. It is, however, a technical piece, and its main purpose is to demonstrate a technique of "marital therapy", i.e., of helping with emotional conflicts that are felt to be destroying the relationship and the persistence of which indicates that the couple cannot overcome them without outside help. Such a therapeutic technique has a further usefulness; it provides unique opportunities to observe and understand the processes of marital interaction. Indeed, the deeper understanding of such intimate relationships and of individual personalities can only be gained in the context of a professional relationship with those who seek help for their suffering. Only under these conditions can access be gained to the inner psychological forces that make for the conflictual, as well as for the more fruitful, aspects of this close relationship.

Marriage makes possible an interaction of two personalities at greater depth and intimacy than is possible in any other relationships except those in early childhood. For the individual, it recapitulates much from past experience, perpetuating the security and goodness of childhood relationships while providing opportunity for their intimate enjoyment to be transformed from immature and dependent modes of gratification into the give-and-take of an interdependent relationship. For these reasons, marriage has great potentialities for psychological and biological growth and for creative attainment. It offers an opportunity for self-realization through relationship with others, which can come from no other kind of personal involvement except, perhaps, from vocation in its fullest sense.

Within the family, of which the marital relationship is the core, the past is recapitulated. Thus, this broader reproductive cycle ensures that what has proved socially useful in self-expression, and in personal transactions, is transmitted through succeeding generations. That it fulfils this function effectively is essential for the adjustment of the individual and for the stability of society as a whole. As Wilson (1949) has said, the family is the primary school in which human relations are learned. It provides the setting within which the crude impulses of infancy and childhood are regulated and, by constructive experience and example, transformed from self-centred need gratification to the give-and-take of mature social interaction.

The fundamental role of a permanent marriage relationship for the individual, as well as for society, is indicated on the one hand by the existence of lasting unions in those societies where promiscuity is permitted, and on the other hand by the historical evidence that instability of marriage and family life coincide with lack of vigour and integration in the community as a whole.

In myths and in the rituals of primitive societies this psychobiological reproductive function of marriage is clearly recognized and is "built into" the economic life of the community and into the reproductive cycle of nature. The beliefs and customs evolved to explain and regulate the beneficent forces of nature that give

security, warmth, and food, and the hostile elements that destroy or
deny such goodness, are often applied also to regulate marital relationships. Codes of behaviour are no less rigorously applied in the
one than in the other areas of life. The change from this kind of
social organization, in which man's primary tasks—the psychobiological and economical—are closely interwoven to modern
social systems in which they are more separate, has added to, rather
than diminished, the importance of nurturing offspring who can
adapt to rapidly changing conditions.

The quality of marital relationships, and what is required of
them by the partners, are influenced by the presence or absence of
supportive or complementary opportunities for social satisfaction in
work and other areas of the community life. Thus, the marital relationship is especially vulnerable to insecurities and pressures from
the changing social organization of which it is an integral part.
Many writers have shown how the degree of social segregation or
isolation of the married couple affects the kind and quality of
demands that each makes upon the other within the marriage; how
supports and satisfactions that are normally provided by participation in wider social and kinship networks are sought, and often not
found within the resources of marriage; how technological advances
have resulted in diminished opportunities for social participation
and for social satisfaction in work life, and have brought about a
separation of work from social and family life, thus producing frustrations that have repercussions upon the marriage, as well as
removing supports that otherwise might have enriched it.

In the past, many interwoven social networks and the closer
contact of work, apprenticeship, and family life provided a continuity of experience wherein relatively homogeneous value systems
ordered the human relationships in all areas of community life. The
fragmentation of modern urban society, with the consequent break-
up of kinship, religious, and social fellowships, puts a greater onus
on the marriage to provide the emotional securities and satisfactions that formerly came from these other closely-knit relationships.

Thus, the family has to provide emotional satisfactions and to
contain emotional tensions, which formerly could find expression
through other social channels, while at the same time it lacks those
kinship and social supports that might have sustained it. This
means that marriage becomes for many people the chief source of

their emotional satisfaction, which in itself is both a danger and a challenge to the further development of the relationship; as Wilson (1949) notes, under modern urban conditions too much emotional current is directed into the marital relationship, which may create stresses and conflicts for the partners and also for their children.

Whereas in communities that were more closely knit in kinship and social and economic transactions and in which satisfactions through direct interpersonal relations were more widely spread, in modern society the need for these satisfactions tends to be directed much more into the marriage relationship (the term "marriage" includes the more modern term, "partnership"). Such increased demands on the marriage to offset lack of personal satisfactions outside it may well increase the likelihood of frustration and conflict. At the same time, modern social and economic life provides opportunities for greater sharing and interchange of roles for husband and wife, and thus can make for a fuller and richer life within the union.

This may explain the growing interest in marriage during the present decade, and the considerable effort to develop services to help marriages in difficulty. The increasingly prominent incidence of marital problems has coincided with a greater readiness on the part of the community and of the individual to seek and accept help for a relationship, which hitherto has been regarded as too intimate to bear outside observation or intervention.

This readiness to provide help and to seek it springs partly from the gradual assimilation within the community of knowledge about the nature and importance of intimate family relationships, which has come about through the infiltration into so many areas of contemporary life of analytic concepts and ideas about personality development.

In particular, experience in Child Guidance and in the treatment of delinquency has shown how severe tensions within the marital relationship, or family breakdown, relate closely to social maladjustment in children. The increased awareness of the unconscious determinants of such tensions, and of the early origins of the feelings of frustration, irrational wishes, and anxiety they engender, has brought about a greater willingness to explore the deeper aspects of marital interaction. The more open recognition of, and more tolerant attitude to, sexual feelings and functions has also made possible a easier acceptance by both therapist and client of the sexual components in marital conflict.

Coincident with the increased need for treatment for disturbed marital relationships, and the related changes in social attitudes and knowledge, new concepts have been developed in the social sciences and in preventive mental health work that are particularly apposite in understanding interpersonal relationships and their conflict. The emphasis has moved from attention to the individual and his capacity for relations with others to a concern with the kinds of interaction that can exist within various social units, be they two-person, three-person, or larger groups.

The health and success of such social units, e.g., the work group or the family group, depends on the interaction between its individual members rather than on the separate contributions of these individuals. This pattern of interaction can be understood only in the context of an ongoing process, which would not exist without the social unit with its own particular purpose.

The parent–child relationship, the family triad, and the marital relationship may be thought of as particular instances of such social units. Their primary task is more fundamental than that of any other social unit, by reason of the extent and depth of psychological involvement required to fulfil it. Since the marital relationship has a double function, the self-realization of husband and wife and the social development of their children, the understanding of its interactions as an ongoing process is of particular importance for the development of preventive mental health work.

In our study of marriage we are concerned with two primary social units: first, that of the families of origin in which each marital partner has built up his own individual patterns of conducting relationships; second, that of the marriage itself, which (like any other relationship, though more directly because of the closeness of its ties) repeats and develops these patterns that were learned during the formative years of childhood. Marriage and the parent–child relationship, more than any other areas of living, focus attention on the over-riding importance of a permanent ongoing relationship as a prerequisite for the healthy unfolding of personality, in adulthood as well as in the dependent period of childhood.

In order to understand marital interaction in terms of these related, though different, primary relationships, and to understand also the nature of the conflicts that threaten the inherent securities and potentialities for growth in marriage, the Tavistock Institute of Marital Studies (now known as the Tavistock Centre for Couple Relationships) has drawn considerably on psychoanalytic knowledge and experience. For the aim of this approach is to understand how early experiences may be superimposed on the more mature marriage relationship, leading, on the one hand, to conflict despite the conscious strivings of both partners, and on the other, in more fortunate conditions, or with suitable help, to an enrichment of the marriage in the depth of its fellowship and mutual fulfilment. It is from such understanding that the method of therapy described here has developed. Its aim is not so much to produce changes in the personalities of the individual partners as to enable them together to make use of the potentialities for growth and self-realization that are inherent in the marital union.

Analytic studies have shown how the relationships that are established between parent and child set the pattern for the making of future relationships, and how unresolved conflicts from this early experience reduce the capacity of individuals in later life to build up mutually satisfying relationships. These studies have demonstrated the importance of unconscious factors in making and maintaining relationships, and they have shown how these centres of conflict arise in the early dependent relationships of childhood. From this knowledge of how they arise, it is possible to understand something of the reasons why the conflictual and seemingly irrational behaviour in more adult relationships is so difficult to influence, in spite of the individual's wish to set it aside.

The most important determining factor in the early phases of development is the child's dependence upon his parents, whom he needs not only for physical survival but who are also the most important objects in his world. The quality of his relations with them determine the security and satisfaction with which he involves himself with his external world. From the beginning of life the basic need of the individual, as part of a psycho-social unit, is to maintain good relations with his objects, specifically people with whom he has close emotional ties, for only by doing so can he feel secure within himself and interact successfully with others.

The intense primary relations of childhood are experienced and lived through when the child's capacity for seeing the world as it is, and for testing out its opportunities and frustrations, is very limited. What is experienced in its reality and what is tested out and assimilated as a body of secure knowledge by the child develops rapidly, though precariously, throughout the early years. This is particularly so in his perception and experience of people, for his dependence upon them and the intensity of his feelings in response to them so frequently tend to distort what measure of real experience he has built up. For example, on occasions when a mother has to punish or frustrate him, she may be felt and seen as utterly bad and threatening. In face of such frustration the child may regress to less mature ways of responding to his objects, losing for the time being, in his rage or anxiety, the secure knowledge he has of them.

During these early dependent phases of childhood, a large proportion of all perception and experience is unconscious in the sense that it includes only a measure of tested-out and assimilated experience of reality, which is proportionate to the gradual unfolding of the individual's capacities. In the normal course of development, such experience, often repeated, gradually approximates to what is valid and secure knowledge appropriate to each phase of growing up.

As such it provides a reliable basis for the extension of experiences by the use of new capacities as they mature, and of knowledge and skills already tried, to extend and enrich his interaction with the individual's world.

This growing body of more conscious, reality-tested experience is organized into what may be called the central ego; it incorporates tried-out and well-assimilated patterns of response and interaction, structured basically in terms of primary relationships between parents and child. Because it is tried out and tested against reality, it has much in common with the central ego experiences of others and thus affords a basis of secure relations with them. The extent to which the central ego is capable of maturation, through the dependent relationships of childhood to the more interdependent personal transactions of adult life, varies with the degree to which it has achieved integration through relationships with objects (e.g., parents) who have consistently confirmed their goodness and secure tolerance of the child's intense and immature ways of self expression.

If the child's experience of frustration from his primary objects is greater than his capacity to deal with them on a reality level, the intensity of feeling engendered is so great that it may override the already assimilated experience of reality. It may threaten to over-whelm completely the resources of the central ego and negate the knowledge of goodness and security in the object relationships already built up. In such circumstances the object is perceived as completely bad, and responded to with feelings, and impulses to action, that express hate or the wish to attack, destroy, or dominate. In extreme instances the child may turn away in apathy and hope-lessness.

In order to preserve that portion of the central ego that is hereby threatened, as well as to preserve the external good objects (e.g., the parents concerned), both of which are essential to the biological and psychological integrity of the child, these intense, negative experi-ences are split off and repressed. With these unconscious sub-systems, some remnants of ego (reality-tested experience) may also be repressed. These primitive, fixated parts of the ego retain their own drives and attempt to serve their own irrational aims.

It is these latter split-off substructures of personality, which are in varying degree unconscious and therefore not accessible to the central ego for the more healthy process of reality testing and reas-similation that produce conflictual relationships.

Even though repressed, these psychological systems are forever active, and, as it were, seeking resolution of the original dilemma from which they sprang. This dilemma consists essentially of the contradictory and irreconcilable perceptions of the needed object; on the one hand that it is good and to be preserved as the *sine qua non* of a secure unfolding of the central ego, and, on the other hand, that it is bad and frustrating, and to be attacked or forced to conform to the blind untempered demands of the immature child. In order to make more full and secure the central ego's experience of its object world, and to reabsorb those resources of personality that are invested in these unconscious split-off systems, repeated efforts are made to test the conflictual phantasy assumptions they contain. Where the strength and security of the central ego is equal to the task, where some linkages between it and the unconscious system can be established, and where the subsequent experience of the object tends to disprove these phantasy assumptions, a good deal of reintegration may be achieved. This is particularly so within the close dependent relationships of childhood (and as we shall see also in subsequent intimate relationships) where the parents can tolerate this repeated testing-out, and where their tolerant and objective responses to regressive behaviour can disprove the phantasy that is the main cause of anxiety; i.e., that the wished-for destructive, hateful relationship will destroy for ever the needed good relationships. The dilemma that arises from this regressive testing-out manifests itself, therefore, as an effort by the total personality to maintain and extend its experience of, and capacity for, good relationships, while in contradictory fashion a part of the personality still seeks irrationally and compulsively to obtain gratification by destructive efforts that threaten the control systems of the central ego. This process of regressive testing-out is seen, therefore, as an important part of the growth of the individual's capacity for increasingly mature relationships.

As would be expected, the testing out and building up of ways of conducting relationships in infancy and childhood centre around those issues that are predominant for both parent and child at successive phases of development. By the same reasoning, later conflictual behaviour, motivated from the split-off unconscious systems of the personality, is typified by the quality and aim of object relationships, which derive from the period in the child's development when the original conflicts were produced. Three important phases in the formative years of infancy and childhood are commonly distinguished in psychoanalytic studies. There is considerable overlap between them, and the transition from one to another succeeding phase will vary in its spacing according to the experience and rate of maturation of the individual child. These phases cover approximately from birth to one year, from one to three years, and from three to six years. It will be recognized that during the first year the intensity of feeling and degree of undifferentiated response to experience is at its greatest. At the same time, the capacity to perceive and assimilate reality is at its lowest. It is only gradually and somewhat precariously that a more secure balance is attained, towards the end of the third phase. Henceforward, a more sure-footed testing-out of reality experience is possible, wherein the patterns of making relationships already learned are consolidated before the psychobiological changes of adolescence that mark the transition to adulthood.

In the first of these phases of the infant's development its contact with the mother is overwhelmingly its most important relationship with the external world. In fact, because the infant is incapable of differentiating between what is itself and what is outside, at this stage, this relationship is its world. The main concern in this relationship is the satisfaction of the infant's need for food as well as for the closeness and wholeness, which contact with the mother provides. The infant is completely dependent, and the satisfaction of his needs is thus a one-way process. On the part of the child it is all taking and no giving; on the part of the mother it is all giving and no taking (though it may be experienced by her, of course, quite differently). The sense of well-being or of total discomfort that the infant experiences according to whether these conditions are satisfactory or not, tends to be an all-or-nothing response in which the infant feels itself and its world to be entirely good, or entirely bad. Its response tends to be an undifferentiated psychological response of the whole organism.

According to analytical findings that are very much supported by infant observation, the child begins to develop the capacity to be aware of and to tolerate a measure of psychological separation from its object (the mother) at about the time when it is also able to achieve a measure of biological independence; i.e., at around the stage of weaning, towards the end of this first phase of development. The infant becomes dimly aware of what is inside itself, its own very undifferentiated state of being, and what is outside, what is self and what is object. The possibility of making a relationship has unfolded, and with it the nuclear structure of the central ego. Here is the beginning of a two-way process in experiencing and testing out relationships with its objects, though it is still very heavily weighted on getting and receiving from, rather than on giving to, the other. Intense greed at moments of frustration (which may depend as much or more on the state of the organism as on the giving of the mother) now constitutes a problem in human relationships. For, with the awareness of the mother as a separate person, such intense greed may devour and destroy the object that is most anxiously needed and that, in its goodness when it satisfies, constitutes the cornerstone of the infant's self, its central ego. To avoid such eventualities, some of this intense phantasy experience may be split off and repressed. It may remain so, or be retested and reintegrated into the experience of the central ego, depending on the intensity and degree of repression and the extent to which subsequent relations with the object tend to confirm or disprove the infant's fears.

At this time, because of the infant's extreme uncertainty as to what is self and what is object, it is normally unable to distinguish clearly whether or not feelings within itself are not also the feelings and attitudes of the external world. At times of frustration, intensity of feeling overrides what little capacity the infant has attained for making this distinction, and it may ascribe its own feelings entirely to its object and, following a splitting-off of such experience, continue to do so in unconscious, though ever active, perception.

Those systems of the future personality that embody unconscious object relationships from this "oral" phase of development will show some of these characteristics when they are superimposed on later relationships, in the efforts of the total personality to attain (belatedly) fuller integration.

The second phase of development in childhood is typified by the child's growing awareness of himself, particularly in terms of his increased capacity in bodily functions and in achieving control of them. The attainment of the ability to walk and to talk brings a greater possibility of communication with his objects and with it a greater capacity to control them and make demands upon them. The intensity of feeling at times of frustration may again make these wishes to control and demand from objects a frightening and conflictual experience, so that repression of these impulses is required. The parents' own value judgements, as well as their personal tolerance of physical demands and aggressions, play an important part in the child's learning of what is good or what is dangerous in the eyes of his objects. This, too, is the age at which toilet training becomes an important issue in the relationship between child and parent. While the child is now, for the first time, becoming more surely aware of self and object as separate, he is at the same time learning the rudiments of give and take in his relations with his parents. Since his awareness of himself is so much in terms of his whole body, he tends to equate it with his conception of self both for himself and for his object—so that the products of his body become important to him in this rudimentary give and take. That they are acceptable means that he is good: that they are regarded as dirty and bad means that he is bad. Intense frustration may again override his clear distinction of good and bad in himself, and in his parents, and he may regard the products of his bodily functions as responsible for making himself wholly bad and dangerous to his parents as, on the other hand, they make his parents seem intolerably bad and persecuting to himself. The danger might be that this mechanism of projective identification may become a fixed, as distinct from a temporary, mechanism in conducting relationships.

By the time of the third phase of development, the child's capacity for perceiving his world more realistically has become greater. His intellectual resources have considerably developed. He has extended the range of people with whom he makes contact and he can become more fully involved with them. He is less dependent upon the mother and more aware of the three-person relationship situation (which includes the father) of which he is part. This phase, then, is typified by the child's growing awareness of the differences between mother and father and brother and sister, both as objects who satisfy important needs in his development and also as people of like and different sex to himself. The awareness of physical differences inevitably rouses curiosity and anxiety about his own body and that of the opposite sex. The curiosity about the nature of sexual differences and sexual functions will be the more securely explored the more the conflicts concerning control of bodily functions in the previous phase of development were resolved.

The child's understanding of sexual differences will depend in large measure not only upon the tolerance of the parents in regard to his explorations, but also on the manner and security with which their own heterosexual roles are taken. From his experience of them he will work out his own heterosexual identifications and build up attitudes about the goodness and badness of his sexual wishes, which may considerably influence his making of future relationships.

The conflicts of this phase are the more difficult because of the intrusion and effect of the child's developing sexual impulses. These are directed mainly towards the parents, and the feeling of rivalry and jealousy arising from his perception that they together have a relationship in which he cannot share. The intensity of feeling when the rivalry dilemma becomes too great may result in phantasies in which he strives to separate the parents, to destroy one or the other so that he may possess one for himself alone, to take the place of one or the other or to achieve a sexual relationship by aggressive and sadistic dominance. A further aspect of this anxiety is the damage that he imagines may be done to him in retaliation for his own destructive phantasies. The anxieties that relate to such phantasies are considerable, for they involve not only the loving preservation of mother and father, but also the preservation of the family unit that provides the secure social base essential for the child's growth towards adulthood.

In so far as he is able to resolve these conflicts and explore the reality of the triangular situation, he will make good use of this important phase of learning human relationships. The child may identify securely with the parent of his or her own sex and accept, and feel accepted by, the parent of the opposite sex; but residues of these conflicts and the resultant confusion about masculine and feminine roles may show throughout life.

The child's capacity to deal with these problems of heterosexual identifications, and the resulting feelings about the goodness or badness of sexuality as a mode of self-expression in interpersonal relationships, has important repercussions on the future capacity of the individual to be a confident husband and father, wife and mother, and to express his or her own loving feelings in the sexual life of a marriage.

It will be apparent that each succeeding phase of development is attempted with the psychological equipment built up in the previous phases. This equipment includes what has been tested out at the level of reality integration appropriate to the child's stage of maturation, and it includes also those areas of the personality not yet so developed or even, in varying degree, split off, as previously described, and therefore less capable of integration into the personality as a whole.

Each phase provides an opportunity for the child's reintegration and consolidation as well as a challenge to move forward to fuller and more reality-based relations with his objects. In a sense, each new phase in the maturation process is potentially something of a crisis, as any big adjustment to new opportunities is even in later life. Insecurity and lack of integration from previous experience produces uncertainty in effort and the likelihood of regression to easier, proven methods of dealing with such situations, even though these methods are now inappropriate to the new stage of maturation. These regressions, particularly in childhood, but also in later intimate dependent relationships, may provide the opportunity to retest what was still insecure, untested, or even split off from the central ego development. Indeed, such regression in childhood is an essential part of the growth process, and is healthy, though upsetting in the intensity of feeling and demand it makes on the object, and in the temporary insecurity and anxiety it produces in the child. It will be healthy and growth-producing to the extent that the parents can tolerate it and help the child to retest his unreal perceptions and irrational wishes against the reality of the situation and of the relationships involved. On the other hand, these regressions in less supporting circumstances, such as when the adult cannot tolerate such primitive behaviour and by his own anxiety confirms that of the child, or when the child's unconscious expectancies are otherwise confirmed, may undo such links as remain between the central ego and the split-off, unformed segments of the personality. Such experience may even consolidate the repressed phantasies and make them impossible to retest, except through skilled therapeutic intervention.

The degree of security achieved in each phase of development provides the psychological equipment and the motivation to meet further challenges and extend the individual's capacity to deal with his world. Throughout the individual's life there are possibilities for growth and reintegration, as well as for regression and rigidity, which will consolidate the conflicting organizations of the personality.

In later relations, as in childhood, the essential motivation of the personality is to achieve a greater integration of the previous experience of relations with people; to bring together the more reality-tested experience of these objects, which we have called the central ego, with those unconscious but ever-active residues of experience that are grossly self-centred, destructive, and controlling, and thereby irreconcilable with the more mature aims of a give and take relationship. Not only is there considerable emotional investment in these latter, split-off, dissociated "systems" of the personality, and therefore less deep feeling available for constructive relationships, but, in varying measures, some of the resources of the central ego are taken up in controlling them in order to prevent their destructive, irrational aims being brought out in reality.

It will be apparent, therefore, that the balance of forces invested in these potentially conflictual systems of the personality, as against those resources available in the central ego, determines whether repressive and defensive, or more constructive, relationships with people are possible.

In a two-person interaction, for example, such possibilities vary according to the circumstances in which the relationship is being attempted, and the conscious and unconscious meanings attached by each individual to the behaviour of the other. Whether the interaction is conflictual, defensive, or creative depends on what is sought by each, on what is offered, and on what is consciously or unconsciously avoided.

Where the areas of conflict in parent and child coincide, or in some important aspect complement each other, it is as if both unconsciously conspire together to ensure that the unresolved residues of unconscious experience that they share is never brought to light to be tested out again in their relationship. For example, the child's repression of phantasy experience, in which he sought to attack or control the mother with the contents of his body, may have the defences he has built up to guard against this eventuality strengthened by the mother's obsessional concern over cleanliness (reflecting some similar residual conflict in herself). The rigidity with which the split-off phantasy relations are prevented from finding any measure of direct expression so that they may be brought into the relationship, retested, and integrated in central ego experience is thereby considerably increased. If the degree of conflict is great in proportion to the total resources of the central ego, there may be little freedom and security to conduct creative and mutually satisfying relationships. If, on the other hand, the degree of conflict involves fewer of the total personality resources, this "collusive" interaction, in which the defences of the mother lend support to the needed defences of the child, may in fact result in increased freedom of self-expression in other non-conflictual areas of their lives.

There is considerable variation in the ways in which these unconscious "collusions" have a restrictive, a creative, or a conflict-producing function in regulating the interaction between two or more closely tied individuals. For example, a "fit" in the restrictive ways by which each married partner regulates unconscious greedy impulses may provide a mutual security by the side of which many other satisfactions may be shared. If, however, the intensity of impulse is very great in one or both partners, the restriction may spread over too wide an area of the marriage and conflict will result.

Many other examples will emerge in the context of the adult marriage relationship from the case studies presented in later chapters. There, also, a great deal of attention will be focused on patterns of interaction where the "collusive" relationships do not fulfil their defensive purpose, or where they do not allow the partners a sufficient measure of creative outlet. In these cases they intensify conflict within the marriage. This may be because the collusion is so overwhelmingly repressive that it denies one or both partners a necessary measure of self-regard or self-realization in their respective roles of husband and wife (as of parent and child). In some cases the taking of heterosexual roles may be greatly restricted in direct expression as well as more indirectly throughout family life. In other cases the "collusion" may provide a mutually needed system of regulation in one key area of the relationship, only to leave some other deeply pressing aspect uncontrolled.

So far we have concentrated on the process of conflict and self-realization within the primary relationships of the family, and our attention has been directed more closely to the viewpoint of the child than to the part of the parent. It will be recognized, however, that within the parent–child relationship the opportunities for readaptation and growth in capacity for making object relations is not all on the side of the child. Where the balance of forces within the interaction permits of security and tolerance for the continued process of testing-out, increased freedoms and forms of self-expression will also be achieved by the parents. It is only when the conflict between the hateful and destructive relationships in unconscious systems and the need to preserve loving, good object relations becomes too great to be tested out within the resources of the two or three persons concerned that the twin process of conflict and growth cannot be contained within the primary relationship. In these circumstances mutual regression and intolerance may result, which threaten the securities on which the primary relationship is founded. So it is in the marital relationship as it was in the earlier parent–child relationship.

The later phases of childhood provide opportunities by which the pattern of making and maintaining relationships that was built up in the early dependent phases may be modified or, in varying ways, consolidated, depending upon the experience within the family and with an increasing range of people outside it. The extent to which these opportunities are used for the creative integration of the personality, and for the differentiation of effective defensive ways of making relations whereby the central ego mediates the expression of unconscious systems in socially acceptable modes of behaviour, depends largely upon the amount of security and tolerance within which social learning has been possible in earlier years. It depends also upon the kind and quality of relations with people that are possible outside the immediate family circle. In modern times, the lack of integration of family, work, and social life that should provide the mores and the motivation for the use of more specific educational opportunities takes away much from the potentialities within these years for growth and consolidation. The pressure to test out increasing physical and intellectual resources with contemporaries in a social context that embodies, and is seen to embody, secure value systems and standards of behaviour is focused too narrowly, and too separately, upon the home and the school. In addition, modern life provides a considerably more direct and wider range of intellectual and emotionally charged stimulation without the opportunity to test out "on the pulses", as it were, its implications for the individual in his relations with his fellows. This stimulation, rich in intellectual and emotional challenge, often carries human relationship implications that conflict with the value systems embodied in family life, and that indeed support rather than modify the direct expression of impulses so typical of childhood. Thereby, also, the conflicts inherent in unconscious systems of the personality are fed and intensified, making the retesting of their irrational assumptions inside and outside the family more difficult. These difficulties, together with a lack of opportunity for integrative experience within the social and cultural networks outside the home, make for a regressive and over-dependent reliance upon the immediate family circle, instead of affording a long phase of exploration in which the learned patterns of conducting relations are extended and consolidated before facing the challenges of adolescence.

Thus, modern conditions present particular difficulties in the way of establishing a secure belongingness within the family and at the same time a basis for a like sense of more independent belongingness in the world at large, both of which attainments are prerequisites for healthy development through the transitional phase before adulthood.

But these discrepancies within the social milieu of the adolescent, the more direct presentation of opportunities for economic independence and for heterosexual gratification, by the side of a lack of integrative supports within the community, have sharper repercussions during this latter phase of maturation. For at this time the child quickly develops physical, emotional, and intellectual resources, which for their fulfilment require him to discover ways of self-expression that conform to adult roles in economic and heterosexual relations. In this transition phase, which involves the giving up of much of the earlier dependent relations and the transforming of them into more mature, independent relations, a great many of the conflicts inherent in each earlier stage of dependence are reactivated. For, in each earlier stage, there was a like dilemma involving the choice between a regressive retention of dependent ties, and the giving up of some measure of such satisfaction in order to meet the challenge of a new step towards independence and self realization.

For the parents, the adolescence of their children may produce, in varying degrees, similar conflicts. Earlier in this chapter we posited the importance of collusion between parents and children. The adolescent child may be trying to free itself from restrictive aspects of this collusion and may no longer be prepared to carry some of his parent's projections. This, as well as the first indications of the child's maturing sexuality, may reactivate anxieties in the parents about their own sexuality and thus offer opportunities to review some of the causes of these anxieties. A child's adolescence may well, therefore, become an area for potential conflicts and potential growth in the marriage. On the one hand the parents may wish to retain too large a part of the child's dependence upon them, either because of their own insecurities, or because the movement of the adolescent out of the family presents them with problems of readjustment within their marriage relationship. On the other hand they may be intolerant of the child's dependence because they tend to measure their own achievement in marriage, as individuals and as parents, in terms of the success of their children in attaining adult independence.

For the adolescent, the approach to adulthood is mediated by his experience of the parents in their roles as man and woman, and as husband and wife, not only in their manifest behaviour in these roles but more deeply in the underlying securities or insecurities that determine them. For it is against these deeper attitudes that his own feelings about his sexuality, and its expression as part of a relationship with another person, have been tested out in conscious and unconscious experience.

Sexual maturity holds frightening or reassuring possibilities for the adolescent, depending on the extent to which he has been able to work out constructive, or adequately defensive, methods of regulating his primary dependent needs, because the impulses that he now experiences are of a like order to those that motivated his search for gratification in infancy and childhood. In particular, he is faced with the possibility of realizing, through expression of these impulses, a sexual relationship—a relationship that previously was possible only in imagination on the basis of the knowledge and experience that had come his way, or in phantasy, in so far as such experience had been transformed by unconscious forces into a frightening or destructive possibility. Realization can therefore hold out either the assurance of transforming the sexual experience of the central ego into a satisfying sexual relationship, or the becoming real of phantasy sexual relationships that would be disrupting and destructive in their unconscious aims.

Although the period of adolescence is potentially so conflictual, it contains more possibilities for reintegration and adjustment than any of the previous phases of maturation. Not only has the individual a considerably increased range and depth of emotional response, but he has also greater and more securely established ego resources with which to give his feelings expression in creative effort, thereby realizing his new capacities for empathy and adult identification. The intensity of feeling, which stems largely from the physiological changes of adolescence, stirs the whole range of previous emotional experience, reactivating much that was conflictual as well as much that was deeply satisfying in the dependent phases of infancy and childhood. This provides a new opportunity for a retesting of past dependent relations, including residual unconscious phantasies, in the context of more mature resources and a more adult exchange of experience with parents.

In describing the primary relationship of parents and child, we have inevitably anticipated much that throws light on the essential features of the marital relationship. We have also moved towards a clearer understanding of what is contained in a primary relationship in terms of its purpose and the conditions required to fulfil it. The essential motivation in all intimate relationships is for the individual to achieve a more secure and creative self through securely based and mutually satisfying relations with others, even though this drive may take many apparently contradictory forms.

In the continuity of the parent–child relationship, the conflicts, which arise from the child's dependence upon the parents and the parents involvement with the child, can become an essential part of the growth process. Although the primary relationship of marriage is an adult relationship, it requires for its fulfilment conditions that match in their dynamic significance the inherent features of this earlier primary relationship. The self-realization of each partner in marriage, as man and woman and as father and mother, is possible only through each other. The attainment of this adult interdependence requires a depth and intimacy of involvement from each partner that matches in intensity the exclusive dependent relations of childhood. Sexual impulses, the expression of which are of central importance to the sense of the completeness which each partner seeks in marriage, epitomize, as it were, the primary nature of the feelings that are brought together and shared within the marriage. A condition of their secure and full expression, as of other intimate aspects of the marital relationship, is the sense of belongingness and the assurance of the continuity of the relationship through which the purposes of the marriage, the self-realization of each partner, may be achieved.

These essential features of the marital relationship are the prerequisites of the adjustment, and of the creative interaction, of the two personalities, as were similar conditions in the dependent years of each partner. Because of the importance of each partner to the other, and the basic nature of the needs that each seeks to satisfy in the other, the interaction is also potentially conflictual and likely to reactivate the dilemmas of earlier dependent relationships.

Indeed, as in these earlier phases of growth, some measure of conflictual interaction is necessary, in order that each partner may extend his capacity for good and satisfying relations with the other.

In marriage generally, the more deeply conflictual aspects of the relationship are contained by the central ego resources that each contributes to the relationship in order to preserve the essential purposes of the union and what is experienced as good within it. In many circumstances the secure resources of good relationships within the marriage can make possible the expression of these deeper conflicts in one or both partners, so that the regressive retesting of their false assumptions may be worked through, thereby extending the capacities for adult give and take within the marriage.

When too large a proportion of the resources of the marriage are taken up with keeping out of the relationship the conflicts and potentially destructive residues of earlier experiences, the measure of self-realization possible for the man as husband, and the woman as wife, may be so reduced that the stability of the marriage is threatened. Or, where the ways of regulating the unconscious strivings in each partner do not fit in the manner described earlier in this chapter, anxiety about the security of the relationship may not only seriously limit the interaction between husband and wife but also prompt them to seek outside help.

It is because the potentially destructive systems of relations that are activated are unconscious and therefore inaccessible to attempts to work them out "reasonably" that outside help is necessary for their resolution. To bring them into the normal process of psychological growth that we have described is possible only where these systems are less intense in their dynamic pressure, and where the total ego resources of the individual, or of the marriage as a unit, are proportionately strong in relation to their pressures. In other circumstances the threats to the individual in his relations with his needed object that their full expression might entail are too great for such regressive interaction to be attempted.

The technique of marital therapy developed by the Family Discussion Bureau (formerly known as The Tavistock Institute of Marital Studies, and then the Tavistock Centre for Couple Relationships) attempts to decrease these irrational conflicts that threaten the security of the marriage and obstruct the normal process of growth and self-realization that is inherent in the relationship. The focus in the therapy is the marital relationship and the individual's contribution to it, rather than the problems of the individual partner. That this aim is explicit throughout the course of therapy provides a secure background against which work with the individual clients may progress. It can provide an assurance that the unconscious phantasy relationships that threaten the marriage will not, in fact, destroy it, which is the essential anxiety that prevents the testing out of the phantasies by the partners themselves. On the basis of this implicit assurance it may become possible for the individual clients to test out their phantasies in the quasi-primary relationship, which is offered to them with a member of the professional staff of the Bureau.

Each partner in a marriage that seeks help works with her or his own therapist. The two therapists keep in touch with each other in order to understand the changing state and progress of the interaction in the marriage throughout the course of treatment. At the same time, in their actual work with clients, they are concerned only with what the client brings to the interviews, and more particularly with the kind and quality of relationship the client seeks to make with them. Because the therapeutic relationship has for its purpose the modification of the client's unconscious conflicts with a needed partner in the marriage, it contains the essential motives of a primary relationship, in which dependence and the need for continuity and exclusiveness play an important part. Within this client–therapist relationship there is, therefore, opportunity to see and to some extent to test out the irrational phantasy relations, especially their primitive destructive aspects, before attempting their modification within the marital relationship itself.

This latter step is one of the central aims of the therapeutic work. It seeks to make use of the "therapeutic" or growth potentialities inherent in the marriage to consolidate and extend the opportunities for change that arise from the process of conflict and realization in the client–therapist relationship.

In this brief review of some of the processes through which the individual's capacity to make relationships with people—and with the world at large—is evolved through a full cycle from the dependence of infancy to the interdependence of adult life, we have frequently changed our focus from the child to the parent, or from the parents to the field of forces in the wider social environment. By so doing it is possible to illustrate the complexity of the process of social maturation and to show how stability and continuity, which are essential to the unfolding of personality, depend upon an inter-play of forces between parent and child in the nuclear family in the context of wider social pressures and supports.

These processes of maturation continue throughout life in the further social and personal relationships in which the individual involves himself. In preventive mental health work, therefore, we may with advantage focus on those conflicts in the individual that prevent him from using for his own growth and development the potentialities inherent in the primary social groups of which he is a part. The diagnosis and treatment, *within* the family, the marriage, or the work group, of such conflicts may prove to be more reward-ing than more intensive individual treatment of any member of a social unit.

Note

1. The word "object" is used rather than person; it is a general term for a source of satisfaction of needs, which may not always be a person. It has the advantage of denoting also the unconscious choice and percep-tion of sources of gratification.

CHAPTER FIVE

An approach to marital therapy

Marriage can make possible an interaction of two personalities at greater depth and intimacy than is possible in any other relationship except in early childhood. For this reason it has great potential for psychological and biological growth and for creative achievement, and for the opposite. It offers an opportunity for self-realization through relationship with another that can come from no other kind of personal involvement except, perhaps, from vocation in its fullest sense.

Within the family, of which the marital relationship is the core, the past is recapitulated.

Mr Baker's marriage

Mr Baker's marriage had been unhappy almost from the start, and he had sought help, over the years, from almost every agency and clinic in his area. At the time of the referral he had been married for nine and a half years and had two children, the first conceived before marriage. He complained of his wife's behaviour with other men and of his own headaches and insomnia. His wife complained of her husband's jealousy and suspicion, and of his violence towards her. She had been refusing intercourse for some months and was daily threatening to leave.

Mr Baker was a qualified technician working for a local Board. He had studied for his National Certificate during the marriage, having previously been a labourer. He was thirty-five, his wife twenty-eight, and they had a son of nine and a daughter aged four.

He was a tall, thin man, shabby and untidy with a strong Cockney accent. He seemed nervous and confused, and spoke in an extremely subservient manner. He gave no impression of having the necessary intelligence to qualify for the job he in fact held.

He began by expressing gratitude for my seeing him and called me "Madam". Then he poured out his complaint against his wife. He told me stories of her flirtations with other men, and particularly of her interest in "inferior" men, for instance, dustmen and coalmen. He said she delighted in humiliating him before such people, and added that she had had a bad mother who had had children by several men. He went on and on pouring out these confused stories, endlessly detailed but often mutually contradictory. When I made a comment, however trivial, he immediately returned to his subservient and placatory manner, turning the comment into words of wisdom. "Oh, thank you, Madam. You would advise me to do that, would you, Madam?" After some time I commented on this, and said that he seemed to be trying to pretend to himself that he was already getting a lot of help and advice from me. I said I wondered if he was expecting nothing, and was trying to ward off his disappointment and the anger and despair he would feel about that. I had thought hitherto that he was too nearly deluded to make any actual contact with me, and was surprised when he reacted. He did not answer directly, but left the stories about his wife and began to talk more rationally. He told me he had been discharged from the Army with psychoneurosis, and that between that time and his marriage he had lived with his parents, quarrelling with them most of the time. "I was awful to my mother, I don't know how she stood me," he said. Then he quickly asked if his sessions could be arranged at such times that his employers need not know about them. He was frightened that they would think him neurotic or mad. I said that he seemed very uneasy about what people would find out about him and was perhaps trying to warn me that I might not be able to stand him either. Again he looked at me as if he had heard what I said and seemed relieved by it.

He could not leave without shaking my hand at the door and thanking me warmly.

He opened the next session by saying he had read books on psychology and had tried to explain to his wife why she behaved as she did, but it was of no use. She just wouldn't understand and that made him furious. I said that he was perhaps wondering whether it would make me furious if he just wouldn't understand, or whether he was afraid he would get furious and frustrated when I failed to understand him. Again he seemed relieved, and then asked if he might take notes or be given definite problems to think about between sessions. I said I felt that it was hard for him to bear the slowness and vagueness of our work and that he seemed to be trying to find a way of keeping at bay his frustration and anger about that. This time he replied directly, admitting his impatience and saying desperately that there wasn't much time to spare. He didn't think he could bear the situation much longer.

Then he began to talk, unasked, about his own history. He had been the youngest of six children in a very poor family; his father had had long spells of unemployment. He felt he had always been "picked on", blamed for everything, and made into the family drudge. He said finally that his mother had had a breakdown when he was born, and had been in hospital for six months. He did not know how he had been looked after. "I don't think I was properly fed as I was always going into convalescent homes later on."

Then he suddenly returned to his stories about his wife's behaviour and went on pouring these out until the end of the session. They were of an even more confused nature than those he had told before, stories about sexual depravity of people not connected with his wife, stories about his workmates, and about people he met in the course of his work. Again he shook hands warmly before leaving.

Meanwhile, his wife was being seen by a colleague. The following extracts are taken from her notes.

"Mrs Baker came to her first interview looking drab and untidy though she was a tall and quite nice-looking woman. She seemed to be at the end of her tether and said she had no love left for her husband and could not stay with him much longer. His irrational jealousy and tempers were quite impossible. Everyday he made scenes about nothing, and had recently begun to smash crockery and damage her possessions in his outbursts. He treated her as an inferior and continually accused her of being a 'bad woman'. She said that there was really no point in talking about the marriage. The only problem for her was how to get away, since there were two young children whom she did not want to leave.

"Only because she thought this was wanted, Mrs Baker outlined her own story. She said she had been the younger of two daughters and had been extremely fond of her mother. When she was seven she had gone into hospital with diphtheria and had returned home to be told that her mother had died while she was away. Her father had remarried two years later, but she hated her stepmother and had left home at seventeen. Soon after this, she had had a love affair, but the man had left her after a few months, and she became promiscuous for a time. Then she met her husband and became pregnant by him, and married him as a result. She said that the only time she had had any satisfaction from sexual intercourse was before marriage. My colleague said that Mrs Baker seemed to have experienced a number of desertions in her life, and Mrs B replied that she had felt 'utterly abandoned' when her mother had died. She said her husband had accused her of not being fond enough of the children, but she felt it was wrong to give 'too much love'. She added that he was himself very good with them, and very concerned about the effect the situation in the marriage would have upon them.

"At her second session, Mrs Baker still looked dreary and showed little animation. She reported further scenes at home during the week. Her husband continued to complain that she was interested in everyone except him. She admitted that she could hardly bear him to touch her and felt quite dead sexually. She repeated that she was remaining with him only for the sake of the children, as she did love them, although she could not show it."

My colleague commented on this difficulty in showing love, and then Mrs B said that the only person she had ever wholly loved was her mother. She added, with a rush, that she had learned later (when she was about fourteen) that her mother had not died at the time she had been told this, but had gone off with another man, but this had not made any difference at all to her feelings for her mother. My colleague said gently that Mrs B must have been very upset about this, and that some bit of her must have been very angry with her mother and might perhaps feel very guilty and very muddled about this and about sexuality in general. Mrs B entirely denied the anger, but said with some relief that she always felt herself to be bad sexually. Then, looking a little brighter, she asked if she might bring her little girl next time, as she was "such a lovely, happy child".

After these initial sessions there was a period of anxiety and frustration for both partners and their therapists. Mr Baker came each week and poured out his complaints about his wife, which became wilder and wilder. He was more violent at home and had outbursts in which he hit his wife and smashed china or broke windows. Mrs B seemed more and more depressed and began making plans to leave her husband. Both partners pressed for a joint meeting in which some of the practical issues could be thrashed out, and we finally agreed to arrange this.

At the joint meeting both of them were extremely nervous and at first found it difficult to say anything. Then the husband turned to his wife's therapist and poured out his troubles to her, making a great appeal for support. He claimed that his wife did not love him, and was unbearable. He said he must have a decision one way or the other. Mrs B then became very angry and there was some cross talk between husband and wife in which each demanded from the other promises of absolute love and no other bad behaviour of any kind. The two therapists tried to intervene and to show the couple how difficult they both seemed to find it to bear the ups and downs of marriage, of alternate love and rejection, kindness and anger, but they were not able to listen to remarks of this kind. Mrs B became very upset and said there were no ups and downs as far as she was concerned. She hated her husband all of the time. Then, half weeping, she said she was "absolutely sick of it all" and rushed out of the room and out of the house, despite the fact that the couple had brought their four-year-old daughter with them and she was playing in another room. Mr Baker made no attempt to follow his wife, but simply said "Now you see what she is like. What can you do with a woman like that?" My colleague then withdrew (still hoping to have another word with Mrs B) and almost immediately Mr Baker's mood changed. He began to sob, and continued to do so for some time. I tried to comfort him, and tried also to show him his confused behaviour towards his wife, his great longing for her love and yet his apparent need to see her as hateful and bad. He gradually pulled himself together and, when able to leave, collected his little daughter. With her, he showed himself as quite a different person, considerate, sensitive, and capable.

The joint session opened a new phase. The wife cancelled her next appointment. He came in a very subdued mood. His wild stories and accusations ceased and he became much more consciously worried about himself. He continued to have outbursts of violence at home, but came to me childishly and pathetically to confess these and to beg for help. I tried to make more direct contact with his destructiveness and despair, and to help him recognize his fury with me and with all women who frustrated him and deprived him, but he remained placatory and anxious, and seemed dull and stupid in the extreme. The only subject in which he was much interested was that of getting his wife back into therapy. While he rationalized this by arguing that there was no point in his working at his marital difficulties if she was not doing so too, it was clear that his uneasiness went much deeper.

I tried to show him that his wife, in walking out on her therapist and thus expressing her anger with her and her feeling of being let down, was perhaps expressing these feelings for him too, and that this was what made him so alarmed by her absence. He denied this completely, but, as usual, seemed relieved that it had been said, and then in a half-frightened, half-provocative manner began to report various critical and sneering remarks that his wife had made about their therapy. Always I put these back to him as being partly his own feelings that he was unable to express directly for fear of destroying the relationship that he had made with me. I tried to link this up with the situation within the marriage and to show him his need to drive his wife to do and say things for him.

After a month, Mrs Baker returned to her therapist, and for a short time there was a great improvement in the marriage. Mr B became much calmer and, for the first time, began to try with me to understand his problems. He began to talk about his work as well as his marriage and made it clear that he had great difficulties with colleagues and superiors. He was able to talk about his uncertainties of himself as a man and about his own father, whom he saw as lovable, but weak and pathetic. He talked about his own children, in particular his son, and expressed considerable anxiety about what he was doing to him. In talking of him he told many stories of the boy's curiosity and anxiety about himself and his body. He talked also of his greed, of his tantrums and jealousy, and yet could see the boy's attempts to make amends and to show love. In this way Mr B was gradually able to come to discuss these things in himself.

Mrs Baker, after her return, seemed relieved that she was able to come back and find her therapist still there for her. She, too, began to talk about her husband as a real person with whom she had a relationship and not just a persecutor. She expressed anxiety about her own sexual frigidity, and seemed distressed about her general inability to show warm feelings. She continued to talk of her mother only in idealized terms, always to deny any suggestion of angry feelings about her, and in the same way she refuted any suggestion of anger or frustration in her relationship with her therapist. Towards me she often expressed hostility. During this short period of improvement she had had a birthday and received from her husband two loving birthday cards, one from "Your Husband Alf" and the other from "The Same Bloke Again", which seemed to express some kind of drive on his part to bring to her the contradictory aspects of himself and to have them accepted. Mrs B was indeed touched by this, and for the first time for many months responded affectionately to him.

The "honeymoon" in the Baker family lasted about four weeks, until my colleague was due to go away for her summer holiday, and my holiday was to follow immediately. Both therapists feared that the withdrawal of help at this point might undo all the good that had been done so far in this marriage and, after some discussion, they arranged that each should make herself available to see the other's patient during the holiday period if the Bakers themselves wanted this. At the first interview after Mrs B's therapist's holiday had begun Mr Baker reported a severe domestic upheaval. He said he did not know how the row had started, but it had ended in a fight in which he had broken a window and blacked his wife's eye. She had gone to the police and to her doctor, and was now talking of applying for a separation. I tried to understand with him what had happened—perhaps as a result of his anger at the therapist's apparent lack of concern for them and his uneasiness now that his wife was no longer supported and that he felt that he was not sufficiently controlled. He could make little contribution to this attempt to understand the situation and again seemed very dull and remote. He presented as a frightened and pathetic little boy, wanting forgiveness and love, and wanting to be told that all would be well.

After this scene, things calmed down again, though there was no further movement towards a better relationship. Mr B. continued to come, but seemed quite unable to make any further attempt to understand himself or his marriage. He came like a little boy, begging for instructions. He seemed to understand almost nothing that was said to him and repeatedly said, "I don't think I quite follow that." I accepted his need for support, but tried a little to show him the fear of his anger and destructiveness that lay behind this. He would not admit any reaction to my approaching holiday, always making admirably reasonable remarks about it.

When I went on holiday and my colleague returned, Mrs B came back to her therapist very depressed and unhappy again. She said her husband was as bad as ever and that she was terrified of what would happen during my absence. My colleague spent the whole interview working over with her patient this recurrent theme of abandonment and all the anger and fear that surrounded it for both Bakers.

Mr B's first session after my return was extremely difficult. He kept his overcoat on (it was early September), turned his chair to face away from me and replied to my conventional greeting: "How am I? Frightened. I'm always frightened." I made an attempt to get him to say more and to explain himself, but he sat silently, still turned away from me.

Finally I said that he seemed to be frightened at this minute since he had remained wrapped up and was apparently unable to talk to me. I said that I thought he was very angry with me for going away, and, as always, very frightened of his anger, which he imagined would harm me or, at best, destroy my interest in him. I wondered, too, if a little bit of him was wanting to walk out on me in revenge, and perhaps that is why he kept his coat on. Mr B laughed and relaxed. He denied every word but took off his coat and settled down to tell me what had happened while I had been away.

From this point the character of the work seemed to change. At the next two sessions both partners reported continued scenes and smashing, with the astonishing difference that now the wife was hitting back and smashing things herself, and that the rows ended with tears and reconciliation. The therapist commented upon the ability of the couple to be loving and reparative after the rows, when the hatred had all been shown and there was little left to fear. My colleague tried to explore with Mrs B the relation between her masochism and her sexual difficulties. She said that her patient seemed frightened to think of sex in terms of love, and while unable to allow herself any intercourse with her husband, seemed almost to invite him to beat her. Mrs B said that sex had always seemed to her like an attack. Then she began to cry and said that she could remember the violent quarrelling that had gone on between her own parents. She hastily followed this with further insistence upon her love for her mother and said fortunately her husband had never said bad things about her mother: "If he does, I shall go berserk". My colleague again tried to show her her misery about her mother's behaviour and her denial of any feelings. For the first time Mrs Baker was then able to express some of her shame and anger.

After this the violence subsided. The couple resumed sexual intercourse after almost a year during which the wife had completely refused it, and the removal of this frustration, and of the utter rejection and condemnation of his sexuality that it had meant to Mr B helped him very much. They were both able to tolerate the fact that it was not immediately very satisfactory. Mrs B began to come to life in the marriage, and the couple started sharing activities and taking the children out together. When they quarrelled it was on a realistic level, as a result of genuine grievances that they had against each other. The wife seemed to be able to stand up for herself more while, at the same time, doing less to provoke her husband's phantasies. He seemed able to see his wife again as a real person and to relate to her as such. He was able to look at some of the projections he had made and understand some of his behaviour in the marriage—his very great demands, his fury when he was rejected, his terror about this, and also his need to see his wife as bad and dirty just because she was his sexual partner. At this stage he dropped both his servile manner and his pathetic childish stupidity and began to show in his sessions the intelligence and ability that had been so hidden before. His appearance changed remarkably and he began to look like a pleasant and capable man.

This couple continued to attend weekly for several months, then asked if they could come fortnightly, and later, monthly. By this time it seemed that they had found ways of giving some support and satisfaction to each other and were taking pleasure in their children's developments and activities. Their internal tensions seemed to have been partly relieved and it seemed that the much freer and more realistic relationship that they had now established might be able to absorb and contain these anxieties in the future. The pressure might at some time mount up again, but it seemed almost certain that the couple would be able to avail themselves of further therapy if the situation in the family showed signs of deterioration.

CHAPTER SIX

Working with a couple

There are as many patterns of marriage as there are individual people. The couple to whom I wish to refer now is one of many. They are involved, on the one hand, in longing to realize with the marriage partner their idealized image of complete oneness, while, on the other hand, feeling swamped and suffocated, and striving towards a more realistic relationship with its promise of greater fulfilment but involving some separateness, frustration, and pain.

I shall be using the same material both to illustrate this theme, and to supplement some general comments on the Family Discussion Bureau (The Tavistock Institute of Marital Studies, now called The Tavistock Centre for Couple Relationships) therapy that will follow.

Any human situation, and marriage in particular, is very complex indeed. In therapeutic work, however, it is not necessary, even if it were possible, to see *every* aspect of a psychological problem and to work it all through in order to bring about change. This is the more so where the illness becomes accessible to therapy through a very intimate relationship between two people, as in marriage. You will know of many instances where one marriage partner is having treatment and the marriage relationship becomes affected, because any withdrawal of projection engenders some measure of release and, therefore, change. Nevertheless, it is clear that much of the psychological movement that results from individual treatment is, in the first instance, diverted from the marriage relationship into the transference relationship with the therapist, and is apt to reinforce an already existing tendency to maintain the status quo of the marriage.

I hope to show that each of the couples with whom I am concerned here has vested in the other partner *not changing* but remaining as he is while, at the same time, being inhibited and frustrated by this situation. In this sense, a marriage problem is a shared illness as well as a shared attempt at psychological growth and fulfilment that has gone wrong. It is for these reasons that the marriage therapist has found it rewarding to treat both partners simultaneously whenever practicable.

The following is a description, first in the husband's, then in the wife's own words, of a quarrel between them. For reasons of time I have had to omit the history of the marriage and have isolated only one aspect of the complex total picture.

The husband's story: "I am going through a stage of mourning; I have been using my marriage like an apron string. Because of this I have tended to do things when it suited my wife, such as going to bed when she did, and always having the bath water after her. One evening during the week I wanted to go on working when she was going to bed. Later I crept into the bedroom and she said, 'The bath will be cold now.' I prickled. Then she said, 'I hope you won't be too tired to do your work in the morning.' I felt her remarks were designed to deprive me of my liberty. I got cross and said, 'Tut tut.' She leapt out of bed, rushed to the bathroom to dress and said she would go out. Then she went to the kitchen and screamed and screamed. She said I had answered her like a whiplash. Then there were sobs, and she became languid and morose. She said she would go round the bend—she was moaning and twisting her hands—it was very distressing. Perhaps I am an irritant to her, better out of the house."

You will notice that in the husband's account of the incident almost all the irrational behaviour is visited by him on to his wife. Now for the wife's version of the same incident, which I have taken from the notes of the wife's caseworker.

"We had a violent row last Thursday. I had slept on my own Monday,
Tuesday, and Wednesday. On Thursday morning my husband brought
me a cup of tea and said it was cold for him without me and suggested
I come back to his bed. Partly relenting and partly because the children
might think it odd I agreed, but at bedtime he didn't go to bed at the
same time and was ages after me and I was nearly asleep. I made a
sarcastic remark about his being fresh in the morning for work—he
went for me like a whiplash and at one point hit me. Later he hit me
again and I got a bit hysterical and went downstairs. He followed and
the row continued."

You will see that the husband left out the fact that his wife had been
sleeping in another room and that *he* had asked her to come back.
She, on the other hand, omitted to mention *her* attempting to keep
a hold on him by expecting him to share her bedtime and her bath-
water. He did not tell me until many months later that he had hit
his wife, whereas *she* had blocked much of her recollection of her
own extremely disturbed behaviour.

I think this incident is interesting as a demonstration of the
conflicting feelings of both of them about their own and the partner's attempts at some measure of separation, physical in the first
instance. Consciously they only recognize their own attempt at
becoming less involved with the other one and at developing some
boundaries of their own. They need, at this point, to ignore the partner's attempt at doing the same thing. The wife, though acting out
some of her anxiety, distress, and rage about the husband's efforts
to get more separate, rationalizes almost as much as he her real feelings about it. They both repress their own hurt and the hurt they
are causing, and instead revert to renewed efforts to get the partner
back and to hold on to him.

I now want to turn to something I am frequently being asked
about: what it is we actually do in an interview with a patient. I
shall presently be quoting some verbatim material from a later
session with the husband, but first I want to make a few general
remarks. The difficulty, as you will only be too well aware, is that
any passage picked out of its context tends to become distorted and
over-determined. Also, anything at all that is said can be understood in any number of different ways, and therefore one person's
interpretations may be unconvincing to someone else. This would
explain why therapists are so wary of quoting themselves.

You may well get the impression from what follows that the kind of problem the patient verbalizes is not really very different from that of any patient in individual treatment, and this is, on the whole, true. However, since we set out to make the marriage relationship rather than the relationship with the therapist the dynamically important focus, our work is bound to be distinct from individual therapy. While aiming deliberately to concentrate on the marital interaction, I nevertheless try to pay heed to the individual material, i.e., we practise what has been described by Malan as "selective neglect".

There are three main pitfalls in this pattern of working with a marriage that one needs to be constantly aware of: (1) the patient who tries to seduce the therapist into making him an individual patient, into our own baby as it were, by constantly denying and repressing his own share in the joint marriage difficulties; (2) the patient who tries to lure us into making *the partner* into the patient, into the ill and mad one again by attempting to remain unconscious of his own participation in the marital interaction; (3) the patient who tries to trap us into interpreting the partner's behaviour rather than his own so that not only need nothing happen to *him*, but also he can go back home armed with the weapon of his therapist's interpretation concerning the partner. This can be particularly tricky in that our patient knows that the other therapist has told me things concerning his partner, which he himself has not told me. He then presumes that we have some special, almost magical understanding of his partner while failing to realize that I invariably also come to know more about his own role in the marriage and am therefore in less danger of colluding with him.

I now come to the extracts from a session with a husband, but in order to make it meaningful I need to put you briefly in the picture. The husband had spent years doing spasmodic freelance work at home. Although the wife had formally been more than willing to use up what money she owned to subsidize the family income, she had become increasingly resentful. What is more, the husband's presence in the house all day had become a mixed blessing for them both. At this point, he succeeded in getting a well-paid, interesting post outside, but on the very morning he was due to start work the couple clashed. At first they argued but then the wife in her exasperation thrust her hand through a glass panel, cutting herself severely. I saw him the next day, and the following dialogue ensued.

> Husband (H):   My wife needs me to make love to her, but I can only do it by imagining that she is a stranger.
>
> ES: As if she were a prostitute?
>
> H: Yes, a very good one I might add. But I feel so irritated with her when she says anything serious, what she says and how she says it. It can't be all right for her either because there is nothing of me there.
>
> ES: You seem to humour, patronize, and appease her.
>
> H: Yes, she has always rather played the little girl. I can't take her seriously.
>
> ES: This is a way of your keeping her small and just where she is.
>
> H: She is a dead bore. She has nothing to say, no vitality, no energy. She has found me and the family sufficient. I had tried to explain to her that *she* is not the only one who is suffering and then she put her hand through the window.
>
> ES: Perhaps you cannot allow her anything of her own, not even her own suffering. You tried to talk her out of it, which was a way of attacking her and yet of also of holding on to her.
>
> H: My wife seems to be a child, as if she had no womb even though she has borne me several children. She is very thin and when I first saw her without clothes I shuddered.
>
> ES: You are not yet able to get in touch with your despair about not having been able to make her into a woman, but only into a mother or into a child.

You will notice how this case material illustrates the problem I referred to at the beginning, i.e., the conflict between the desire for complete union with the other and the need to become more separate. The husband conceals from himself his deep involvement with his wife behind a mask of contempt. He attempts to disown her. He experiences her as the prostitute or the little girl and is unable to see her as herself. At the same time he complains that she is not a woman. Thus, he avoids facing the conflict of togetherness and separateness, which is intrinsic to any relationship between a man and a woman, and escapes the depression that belongs to it. At the same time he is frustrated and unfulfilled and longs for a change which, nevertheless, feels too dangerous. So he clings on to an idealized image of oneness with the perfect woman who always eludes him.

The wife, for her part, though struggling desperately to become a person in her own right, inflicts an injury on herself which immobilizes her sufficiently for him to have to rush home from work and to do many of the things *she* would be doing. She, too, has found a way of keeping him tied, and that at the very moment when he has taken some steps to greater independence. Thus, each one imposes on the other a fixed pattern that they can control. This sets up a defence against the uncertainties of the unknown. Invariably, change is equated with loss and intolerable pain.

I should now like to return to a point I raised earlier: the question of what governs me in interpreting material in the way you have heard, when it could be used in many different ways. You may have notice three points particularly, which, from my experience as an analyst, differentiates Tavistock Institute of Marital Studies' (TIMS) work from individual therapy.

First, the frequency, outspokenness, and directness of some of my interpretations, which deal largely with near conscious material. This is, in part a feature of once-weekly interviews as against more frequent sessions, but more important is the fact that, since in most cases *both* partners are in treatment, a great deal of ongoing "therapy" takes place at home. In other words, much of the working out of conflicts is contained within the marriage relationship and the family set-up rather than within the relationship with the therapist.

This leads my to my second point, which is that transference interpretations are employed very much more sparsely in marital work than is usual in individual work. An awareness of transference phenomena is, nevertheless, an indispensable key to any understanding of the material as well as the therapeutic situation.

My final point is not an easy one to convey because, as I see it the orientation of TIMS' interpretations is different from that of a more classical approach. In the extract you have read, for instance, one might have explored the husband's sexual fantasies around prostitutes, or the castration anxieties, both of which are evident in his material. One might have focused one's interpretations on the personal roots of his neurosis. Interpretations, on the other hand, are primarily directed towards the undoing of a complex web of cross projections in a shared illness, and this, it seems to me, is the salient feature of this work.

Any distinctions I have drawn are, of course, relative and not absolute; it would be misleading to profess that we do not at times interpret the transference directly or discuss dream and fantasy material with the patient. In as much as deliberately avoiding doing so, however, we might be thought to be manipulating the psychological material; this I should dispute on the grounds that being purposely selective in psychological work is in any case inevitable, and is therapeutically justified when geared to the marriage situation.

CHAPTER SEVEN

The therapeutic moment: reflections on the importance of freedom of communication

A nalysis, like life, is concerned with communication, but also with boundaries. Both of these determine growth and movement, or else paralysis, stagnation, and despair. For us, as analysts, the problem of communication and of the strengthening of ego boundaries belong together. They constitute a continuing challenge to search for new possibilities, a task that can never be wholly accomplished in any single lifetime or generation.

Furthermore, it is commonplace in the work of a supervisor to find that analysts-in-training, who over-identify with their patients, become stuck in (or even overwhelmed by) the therapeutic alliance. It was as if, initially, the emphasis had been directed towards enabling a regression in order to re-establish contact with the still undamaged, and also with the starved and arrested areas of their psyche. Subsequently, the emphasis became the gradual building up of ego boundaries within which they could begin to integrate and then relate to others as closely as to themselves. The complex pattern of interrelationships between these two complementary processes determines the course of any one analysis, and I shall be bringing some case material later to illustrate the point.

Freudians and Jungians are increasingly in dialogue, discovering areas of common ground. Over the years, each school of analysis had become an integrated system of theory and technique in its own right. The quest, or struggle, for identity is a necessary part of the existence of every person, and every group is giving way to the question that I have already posed. How can we stand apart, and yet enrich our lives by getting to know each other better? Dynamic psychology, as the term implies, is in a constant state of change. Frontiers become blurred; but they are eventually rebuilt. Such is the rhythm of every living process or organism.

For those of us who follow on in analytic practice, this new development and dialogue could mean liberation from a barren conflict of loyalty and allegiance in which much libido has been absorbed in upholding a good enough image of the one or the other parent figure. Instead, the process of differentiation from the parent figures, a fresh assessment of their qualities and limitations, and an exploration of our own individual resources are set in motion. Ultimately, successful analysis depends on whether each one for himself becomes able to evolve and adapt a theoretical framework, which avoids a betrayal or surrender of his unique personality, his experiences, and capacities. To quote Michael Fordham in his article: "The relationship between the ego and the self" (1963): "Theory is understood not as an autonomous impersonal structure on which the analyst bases his technique, but as the abstract expression of the analyst's own self *insofar as he relates to his patients as a whole*" (my italics).

What, then, are the implications of giving up the slender security of parental identifications? First and foremost, it entails the confrontation with an experience familiar to analysts of knowing only in part and of facing some degree of doubt and confusion. The burden of a perpetual search for our own and our patients' truth implies a preparedness to risk experiences of chaos. Like an infant learning to walk, we may frequently shuffle and even fall, but we also learn to pick ourselves up again, and in so doing discover who we are. Surely, the door is opened at that moment when we no longer *have to know*.

I should like to remind you of the famous passage from Chapter 13 of Paul's First Epistle to the Corinthians which begins: "When I was a child . . ." and goes on, "For now we see through a glass, darkly; but *then* face to face: Now I know in part; but then shall I know even as also I am known."

So far, I have stipulated one fundamental basis for communication between people, i.e., the giving up of rigid precepts that suffocate spontaneous development. Whatsoever cuts breaches in the dividing wall is linked to the way we give of ourselves in our life and our work. It is the exploratory, rather than the finalized, attitude that is conducive to contact rather than, as is often supposed, which school of psychology, or which faction of our particular school, we become associated with (often in the eyes of other people rather than in our own view). I feel that, in T. S. Eliot's words, "we may sometimes have been looking for something vital in the wrong places" (Eliot, 1925).

The crucial criteria here are how we, as analysts, deal with defensive systems, with transference phenomena, and with manifestations of anxiety within our patients as well as within ourselves. It is in this fundamental area that I have found similarities, as well as decisive chasms, between analysts of the Jungian and Freudian schools, reflecting important links or divergences of technique that require recognition and elaboration so that the building of bridges can proceed.

This is an area where the garden gate has a rightful place, symbolizing as it does both a separation and the possibility of entry. I should add here that long-term discussions about whether Jungian analysis is concerned with reduction or with synthesis have inevitably been inconclusive, for neither of these two processes can possibly proceed autonomously. Defensive systems, if not analysed and reduced to their origins, produce a split within the personality, which would tend to defy integration. Conversely, the aim of reductive analysis cannot be other than to make possible a reconstellation of psychic forces from which greater wholeness and harmony may result.

The misunderstandings that arise from differing uses of language are, of course, real and relevant to any discussion of problems of communication. Already, much attention has been given to this problem and no doubt it will continue to occupy us. I feel, however, that even if it were possible to devise an Esperanto of the psyche, the problems of meaning will challenge mankind forever. I should like once more to refer you to the Bible: "There are so many

kinds of voices in the world, and none of them is without significa-
tion. Therefore if I know not the meaning of the voice, I shall be
unto him that speaketh a barbarian, and he that speaketh shall be a
barbarian unto me." And later: "I had rather speak five words with
my understanding . . . than ten thousand words in an unknown
tongue."

I shall now leave these more general considerations and turn to
a related topic with which I am preoccupied.

Man is forever attempting to resolve his state of isolation, which
begins at birth. While still inside the mother, he comes closest to a
state of oblivion and merging that he seeks again and again. In this
sense, an individual life can be said to begin when he finds himself
in a state of communion with another person outside the womb,
usually his mother, and, with luck, his father too. One would
suppose that this experience occurs at some time soon after birth,
and that it will become the basis for other forms of communication
throughout life; that is, if the mothering has been sufficiently in
harness with the baby's inherent needs. I am, however, concerned
here with patients where all the available evidence points to this *not*
having been the case. Their histories show a great deal of psychological deprivation and unsatisfactory "feeding" from earliest
infancy onwards, as well as bitter conflicts and violent scenes
between the parents leading, in every case that I have in mind, to
repeated and eventual final separation. Frequently, children
suppose the quarrels to have been about them, so that they feel
responsible for splitting the parents.

It seems to me that the tendency has been for these patients to
disown the needy baby who is a part of them, and thus to abandon
much of their own self and their capacity to communicate with an
external mother figure as well as with other people. They then
retreat to a state of communion with a more anonymous something,
possibly like the womb, or an image approximating to it.

During the process of analysis, a fixation to a state of primary
identity emerges, not so much with the actual mother or an illusory
one, nor even with an external part of her such as her breasts, but
rather with an amorphous entity *inside* her body. They become
enveloped in the idea that being *inside* was the only wholly good
experience they have ever had, i.e., the only time when they
thought of themselves as wanted and valued and therefore safe. It

is significant that this picture is hitched on to a stage in their lives when they can hardly be said to have been themselves, since they were still a part of their mother.

One patient has put it as follows: "I wanted to be born, but the whole thing was a big mistake." He then developed his womb phantasy as follows: "I shall never be free of what I came out from. In the womb, I was delighted by the movement of my mother's heart and blood; it was celestial and timeless like the stars in their orbits. Time seemed to be going on forever." I do not think it will be difficult for you to infer, from this phantasy, a picture of his life situation in which he is predominantly inactive, isolated, paranoid, and despairing, and describes himself as "nothing, useless, sexually impotent, disgusting". In addition, he had been considerably incapacitated by not being able to make proper use of his eyes, which had been several times examined and said to be normal. I felt there was a link here with his womb-like existence. He himself said: "I shall see when I really *want* to see."

In the transference I initially represented the womb, which he could not give up. Some of the time he still continued to be deluded about me in this way. So I did not exist for him as myself. Each and every separation had previously tended to be an experience of death for him. It was only when he first came into my room that he perceived and protested against his realization that I was different and separate from him, and he regularly complained that I was different each day, meaning, "you are different from me". Very soon, he would attempt to re-establish a situation in which he could be sucked back inside. For instance, he would begin the session by asking me what *I* would like *him* to talk about today. If, however, it were to happen, i.e., his being sucked inside, he would show symptoms of suffocation, such as becoming breathless, agitated, and vomiting out my every interpretation.

If, on the other hand, he felt as if pushed out prematurely by me, his rigid defences were aroused. An interpretation that was not carefully enough timed could have this effect on him, but he also frequently did not listen or failed to comprehend what I said to him. When I pointed this out he replied, "I only listen for things that fit in with what I already have." He often told me, in all seriousness, that he could not understand why I did not devote my entire life to *him*, or else he felt that everything I did was determined by *him*.

On one occasion, when I interpreted his wish to be my baby inside me, he said: "I'm glad I'm forming inside you. When this can go no further there will no longer be any point to my existence."

Early on in the analysis, being separate, having boundaries, was synonymous for him with being cast out, distorted, and disgusted, i.e., what had felt good inside had come out as shit. As soon as he felt bad, his paranoid defences were brought into play, and he gave himself and me hell. He could never remember afterwards what happened, because he could not tolerate the memory of a contaminated session, i.e., the womb that had turned bad. At one time he used to run out of the house because he became terrified of physically attacking me—it was only much later that I understood my passive calm, which had felt unnatural, but had enabled him at that time to come back. Nevertheless, I can now see that my lack of response contributed towards my becoming for him an untenable delusion, an indestructible fortress of a womb, immune to his violent, sadistic impulses but also impenetrable to his struggle to become himself. When both he and I were less frightened because he could speak of his sadistic impulses as well as his loving ones, and was no longer so close to acting them out, I could show him more response. Thus he exclaimed, "So you must, after all, think I am real!"

Some weeks previously he had told me that he felt like a ghost who could not die because he had never been born, and that it would have been better if he had been sentenced to solitary confinement at birth. Nevertheless, he sometimes clutched my hand as he left, thus taking with him a small fragment of an experience of communication between us outside the womb. Simultaneously, he began to perceive himself differently in that he was less disgusted by his own image. He became more outgoing with people and was able to use his eyes effectively. He no longer said, as he used to, "I have nothing to do with this world. I don't belong to it."

There are patients who, like him, cling tenaciously to living as if inside the womb, particularly during periods of stress or when they are faced with new departures in their lives outside that threaten them with greater separateness. In time, one learns to distinguish between a patient's real need and an unconscious manipulation, which is intended to avoid the anxiety of growing up. As the ego boundaries become stronger and more flexible, interpretations, which are, after all, communications, become increasingly possible and meaningful.

In this connection I should like to tell you of a dream a depressed woman patient had the night before an important interview, which, if successful, would vastly improve her whole life situation. She dreamed she was in a boat on a sea that was utterly still and unspeakably beautiful. (Incidentally, this image is reminiscent of the other patient's womb phantasy.) The water was transparent, and on the sea-bottom she saw numberless dead trees. She called it the Dead Sea. After a silence, I said, "It seems important to keep your boat afloat." At this she became extremely angry, protesting that it wasn't like that at all. On the contrary, the scene attracted her irresistibly because it meant peace and death at last, and that she only wanted to drown. I felt myself being manipulated into becoming the constricting womb just when her chance to launch out into life was upon her. I responded by being still, calm, and silent. She then complained about how impossible I was to talk to when I was being so unresponsive and discouraging. It seemed I, too, had become for her the Dead Sea, but without its fascination, no longer beckoning her to sink into it and so retreat from life.

Subsequently she was appointed to the post and was able to set up a home of her own for the first time.

There is little doubt that any prolonged collusive response in the analyst could become disastrous. As far as the patient is concerned, he becomes trapped in the celestial womb, which eventually cannot but lead to his psychic death and the renunciation of his struggle for his own identity.

It is noticeable that the patient begins to show signs of deterioration in every area of his life. As for the analyst, a state of isolation would increase the strain of carrying such cases. Communication helps to mediate the burden and becomes to me, at any rate, a vital necessity.

To sum up: communication, which nourishes growth, depends on boundaries. Man's yearning for a state of oblivion, or of total merging, may symbolize his longing for immortality and for escape from his sense of isolation; but, even if this could be achieved, it would produce atrophy, a kind of living death. A productive life requires boundaries; but *the therapeutic moment* is a fleeting one when communion with another person becomes possible.

I end with the wisdom of T. S. Eliot:

> "The awful daring of a moment's surrender which
>   an age of prudence
> Never retracts. By this, and this only, we have existed"
>
> [*The Waste Land*, 1925]

CHAPTER EIGHT

Some thoughts on stagnation and resuscitation in analytic work

P redominantly, the analyst encounters dissociated personalities. His initial task is to be the listener, absorbing fragments
as a tree absorbs the rain, while aware within his own depth
of the potential unity of all life. The task is like a jigsaw puzzle;
patiently, one segment at a time is dealt with. The undertaking can
be perceived like struggling with an infinite number of splinters
that have broken away from what might once have been, or
may eventually become, a whole and continuous personality. With
most patients, the analyst will do well if he pieces the fragments
together by reintegrating some of the lost contents and associating
them with consciousness. Thus, the patient's condition is objecti-
fied and brought into some general connection with mankind and
the human situation. In so linking the individual to the general
human meaning of his particular predicament, he is rescued from
being thrown back totally upon himself, into the isolation of
his illness, his unconnectedness. With the recovery of a lost dimension, the patient may experience his creativity and therewith a
measure of synthesis may be achieved. He can become a person with sufficient consciousness to be a participant in the stream
of life.

I share Jung's view that the analyst should not strive to achieve a radical "cure" in all his patients; experience has taught me that a "rescue operation" is the furthest that one can hope to go with many people, and it is not to be despised. The way to a totality of being is also the path to what is often a hidden and terrible danger. The very location where the jewel of wholeness is embedded is, at one and the same time, the place where the dragon of chaos has his den. The analyst needs to be constantly watchful, and not to impose his goals or his own personality on to his patient. He should rather work with inherited capacities, whatever they may be, and modestly strive to support the other to fulfil himself within his limitations, and to help him to become as whole a human being as is possible for that one particular person, since I have postulated that he may never become whole. From time to time, however, a fitting together of the split-off fragments into a relatively cohesive whole is transcended, and then the terrors of disintegration and chaos may become a transition to rebirth and the beginning of individuation. This search for wholeness often entails near-unendurable experiences of loneliness and apartness.

In a paper read to the Society in 1962, called "The half-alive ones", I described patients who had become stuck in a permanent state of twilight, of non-differentiation (Seligman, 1982). They were characterized by their frozen, sexless, numb, and anonymous personalities. The roots of their condition were traced back to a symbiotic type of entanglement with one of the parents, and I used the term "symbiotic relatedness" in the manner in which Searles had referred to it (Searles, 1961). Symbiosis means a permanent union between organisms, each of which depends for their existence on the other. The challenging question for me at the time consisted of trying to unravel the knot in which the patient and the parent continued to be tied well beyond childhood into adult life. I described patients who had failed to negotiate even the first separation of life, who could not tolerate the abandonment of birth. Jung says, "Child means something evolving towards independence. This it cannot do without detaching itself from its origins; abandonment is therefore a necessary condition . . ." (Jung, 1940), one which the "half-alive" patients had been unable to accept. I had noted that the patients I described could rarely tolerate aggression or be openly aggressive themselves. Occasionally, however, there was an uncontrollable outburst of explosive proportions, which came close to obliterating whomsoever was currently the most important person, a total elimination of the "bad" by shattering it into fragments. But withdrawal, depression, and paranoid splitting reactions were much more observable, an unconscious manoeuvre to control and preserve the status quo. This brought about long periods of stalemate in the analyses when resistance to change bogged down any observable movement. Extensive spells of passivity and hopelessness had to be negotiated, and thus an illusory sense of security and of seemingly self-containment was upheld.

For several years I have continued to remain convinced that the recovery of some of these patients was linked with the rediscovery and reclamation of the second parent as a positive life force. Since, more often than the mother, it was the father who was "missing", I had written of "the role of the father as the mediator in the transition from the womb to the world. To make this tolerable, it needed the participation of both parents". Further, I had said that the "venting of aggression and rebellion against the symbiotic partner, usually the mother, is too dangerous unless the father, the masculine side is experienced as protecting and preserving both partners from the wounds of attack and ultimate separation". I had ended thus: "Healing may consist of re-activating a mother/father constellation, which will ensure survival. The patient's investment in his own development will be restored to him and make him more whole, whereas the symbiotic parent will be compensated by having his or her original partner restored" (Seligman, 1982).

Up to a point, I still stand by these ideas, but have since often come up against the snags and insufficiencies of restricting myself to the child–parental triangle. What follows is a development of my earlier thoughts, based on subsequent experiences with two patients in particular. Salient features of one of these analyses, that of Mr A, will be described in the final section. It demonstrates that the original formulation did not go far enough to explain the bogging-down of analyses even after the "lost" parent has been reinstated.

In recent years I have encountered over and over again a particular encapsulated complex that, at first, appeared to resist further analysis. I reached this point with about a third of my patients of either sex, even when the analyses appeared to have gone well in the earlier phases. Nevertheless, an obstacle arose, an ultimately refractory element, which seemed like an insurmountable impediment to further growth and development. It manifested itself in recurring and ostensibly unexplainable collisions with the actualities of the real world, the patient never feeling quite right, never quite fitting in anywhere; some part of him remained unadapted and infantile. There was a continuously existing core element of despair, and of protest that defied assuagement, a perpetual polarization of the "I" and the world. Some ingredient of the personality appeared to be extinguished and unamenable to psychological resuscitation. The patient was exhausted by the struggle between love and guilt, passion and renunciation, life and death. There was a ceaseless search for inner peace that eluded him, activating a longing for oblivion as the only solution that remained. It was as if the quest for integration, for the re-integration of the fragmented and split-off facets of a personality, could never quite be accomplished.

There are affinities here with a religious experience that has remained unconsummated, and with themes frequently encountered in myths, poetry, and music. The story tends to go something like this: the chief character waits to meet the lover, knowing at the same time that he will not come; he has either deserted him for another or has been snatched away by death. In the renouncing of him, he becomes "transfigured", because the other, the "lover" symbolizes a hitherto undiscovered part of himself with which he becomes re-united, and therefore more whole. An indelible sadness, however, remains.

This motif has much in common with how I still experience some of my patients; their seemingly infinite capacity for accepting suffering without hope of satisfaction and happiness has struck me, and I am not here referring to a masochistic manifestation, which can be analysed. These people feel something of a stranger almost everywhere, as if the pre-natal state from which they have never fully emerged is one into which they long to be absorbed again. As D. H. Lawrence wrote to his mother: "Twice I am born; to life and to death in you. Thus the unborn body of life is hidden within the body of this half-death which we call life" (Lawrence, 1962).

All patients are liable to project into every life situation feelings that originate in their own body image. And it is precisely this, the disturbed body image in these patients, that is the area of "basic fault" (Balint, 1968), of "critical hurt" (Barker, 1972), and which seems to block a resolution within the analytic process. This situation continues to remain pertinent even at the stage when the patient's ego, long denied, mortified, pushed out of sight, progressively comes to assert its right to definition.

I think I may at last have identified the core of this disturbing pattern: these patients have been born the wrong gender and the wrong shape; nature has cast them in the wrong mould. That is, they came into the world as the other gender, not the gender their parents wanted them to be. This is their irremediable encapsulated affliction, and they are struggling in vain, impelled all the time, to solve the insoluble. It is my experience that the most severe damage to sexual and personal development occurs when it is the parent of the same sex who is thwarted and disappointed in the offspring's gender, and it is inconceivable that such disappointment should not have been transmitted to the child in one way or another. Thus, an "accident" of nature becomes the germ of a life-long exhausting conflict. At best it is something that can be accepted. A true synthesis, however, which would lead to individuation, seems difficult to achieve, for it would appear to involve having the physical attributes of both sexes. Indeed, it is no surprise that many of these patients have some noticeably hermaphroditic features.

The basic disability of having been born the "wrong" sex, even when exposed and thus no longer repressed, tends stubbornly to remain. In a sense, the patient is left, forever isolated, imbued with a disturbing element that cannot be absorbed. His haunting impulse is to slink back or to rush forward into the womb of the earth, where male and female were blended before they become separate. These patients are all lovers of nature and animals, of situations in which their being of the wrong sex is no obstacle to their feeling of being accepted. It is my intention to make a statistical study of my analytic cases at the end of twenty years' work in the hope of verifying my hypothesis. My estimate of a third of my patients as having been born the wrong sex, the wrong shape, is based on a review of my current and more recent work, and my endeavour is to make my research as comprehensive as I can.

The corroborating evidence for what appears as an obvious conclusion has evolved over the years from dreams of male and female patients, and their subsequent elucidation. I maintain that I am dealing with an irreducible complex, and not with the well-documented areas of envy of the sibling of the other sex or Oedipal phenomena, nor with Freud's penis envy. In my paper on anorexia nervosa I suggested that patients suffering from this illness were trying to force a change in the shape of their bodies in a futile attempt to simulate the sex that the all-important parent had wished them to be (Seligman, 1976). We are all of us familiar, however, with the conscious recall of early childhood memories of boys being dressed and treated like girls, and vice versa. My proposition is not primarily concerned with this conscious or hearsay material, but it will serve as initial confirmation.

Thus, a man in his middle years, who presented himself as a *puer aeternus* with no recognizable sexual characteristics, had learned from servants at the age of four that his father had longed for a daughter. This man was the middle one of three sons. In the course of his analysis he remembered trying to obscure visual evidence of his penis by squeezing himself into the elasticated sleeping suit of his one-year-old brother, and not being able to get out of the suit until his mother cut it off him! He did his utmost to castrate himself in order to approximate to his father's longing for a girl child. He also used to ransack the laundry bin for his mother's underwear, which he put on. The complicating factor was that, while he disappointed his father, and there was no relationship between them, he was his mother's favourite son, He had tried to maintain a place with each of them by his continuing bisexual appearance and way of life. Yet he continued to grieve for his dead father, with whom he never forged a bond.

A second patient has been weighed down by life-long unexplained daily morning spells of "paralysis" and despair. Eventually he was able to link these to an occurrence of more than sixty years earlier when, aged four, following his father's premature death, his mother had sent him away to boarding school, while keeping his sister at home. Her rationale was that she could not manage a boy, but simultaneously she let it be known at the school that he was delicate and needed indulgence and protection, thus seeing to it that he was barred from the compensatory satisfaction of his maleness.

While his peers played boisterous games, he was asked to dig holes in the ground with a spoon. His recurring "morning gloom" coincided with the time of day when he was initially sent away, which to him had felt like a death sentence.

Yet another patient was the third of four sons; he also was intended to be a daughter. In his early years he was dressed in frilly, pretty, girl's clothing. Aged four, he had a terrifying experience. All of his family, including himself, lived in fear and trembling of his violent father. One teatime my patient stretched his arm across the table, when a vicious blow with a cane wielded by his father struck his right hand. Ever since he has suffered from a severe writing impediment; it takes him about three hours of laborious effort to cover one page of handwriting, and whenever he is under stress this same hand swells up and becomes crippled. In spite of his indelible injury, this patient was the only one of the sons who went to live with his father after his mother's death; at long last he approximated to a daughter's role.

I have chosen these particular male patients because all of them were intended to be female; and this links back to my earlier emphasis on the importance of the "lost" parent, and more particularly, to the significance of the parent of the same sex for the person born the "wrong" sex. It shows the reverse process described in my previous article in which the anorexic girl was trying to be a boy (Seligman, 1976). None of these patients, or others that I have in mind, ever succeed in feeling quite right with anyone, or right in any situation. They could be said to be permanent misfits. The realization that the vagaries of nature are beyond their power has not diminished the unalterable tragedy of their being born the "wrong" shape of the "other" sex. An infinite variety of dreams with mutilation themes occur with these patients. Castration symbols abound. One of the less gruesome, but evocative repetitive dreams was that the dreamer's penis was detachable, and that he could just take it off, hold it in his hand and dispose of it at will. I would emphasize that I am referring to experiences of self-castration aimed at the acquisition of the father's love. My interpretation of castration manifestations differs from Freud's view that castration anxiety is due to rivalry with the father for the mother's favours, as well as from Jung's ideas, which link castration of the son with the archetype of the devouring great mother.

In adulthood it is predictable that if these people achieve a relationship with a member of the other sex, it must be on their own terms, characterized by a search for the other as a mirror, which reflects the inwardly longed for, but outwardly unattainable, body-image. Their requirement of their partner, and of their analyst, is for total, irrational, undemanding adoration, irrespective of their own behaviour. Failure and futility are predetermined.

An encapsulated complex

I should now like to substantiate the material already given by posing some of the questions it raises, and by attempting a more theoretical formulation.

As already stated, my last section will consist of a more detailed account of the analytical process of one particular patient, Mr A, which manifests developments that, happily, contradict some of my more pessimistic predictions.

The reader may wonder whether patients afflicted by what I have called "an encapsulated complex" should be accepted for analysis at all. If so, and if my assumption is right that there is a core damage that defies repair, what then might be acceptable as a good enough outcome? Furthermore, if problems that cannot be resolved inevitably remain, how and when should the analyst aim to terminate these analyses? A more than usually careful assessment of what is, and is not, analysable in people with these particular complexes seems to me to require especially careful scrutiny. If I am right, there is, I believe, room for guarded optimism alongside constant vigilance of restricted, limited goals. While some compensatory developments can take place, other basic wounds remain unhealed.

Some of the ideas expressed by Kohut have seemed relevant to my theme, and have clarified some of the issues, adding new dimensions to well established theories. He focuses on narcissism not only in its pejorative sense, as deleterious to the enjoyment of life and the ability to function, but also as a vital and life-embracing force in the child's development towards maturity (Kohut, 1977).

His ideas have helped me towards a clearer formulation of the affliction that affects those patients described as suffering from "an encapsulated complex". I think of them as having inherited a congenital, malignant, narcissistic illness from one, or the other, or both of their parents. In the first instance, the narcissistic disturbance in the mother will make its impact, producing a faulty response to her baby, and probably a major failure in the primary mother–child relationship. Kohut specifically describes this situation as "flaws in the mirroring functions of the mother".

There is a further complication that I have observed, which is that, in the case of patients born the "wrong" sex, their parents have become overwhelmed by a sense of failure, emptiness, and worthlessness, and it becomes *they* who seek reassurance from their child. Thus, the mirroring function of the mother becomes vested in the child. A reversed child–parent situation is established, engendering not only a sense of inadequacy and unreality in the child, but also life-long despair. It is well beyond him to repair his parents' wounds. Whereas in the course of more or less "normal" development, infantile narcissism is gradually transformed into object-love, this group of patients continue to experience the feeling-states of the parents as if they were their own; the state fusion is perpetuated *ad infinitum,* and can become irreversible. The child's psyche is presented with one of two choices—to remain fused or to wall itself off. Its autonomy is diminished. The overriding desire of the parents for him to be of the "other" sex can never be fulfilled. A sense of his own identity cannot be firmly established, and the terror of losing it altogether haunts him throughout life. In Kohut's words: "the child exchanges direct drive satisfaction for parental approval" (Kohut, 1977). Failure of empathy between parent and child become extensive, culminating in an almost total failure to provide for the child's needs for optimal parental and environmental response.

As a result, patients from such a background often say that a part of them has died; it is then that the periods of stagnation to which I have referred occur in analysis. These cannot be attributed solely to an absence of a minimal life-sustaining matrix for the child's emotional requirements, and for sympathetic responsiveness. I attribute this state of stalemate predominantly to his being unalterably of the "wrong" shape. It has become predictable that only some fragments of his personality are likely to develop with any measure of confidence and effectiveness. In my experience, the area of his maximal functioning is his thinking process, often over-developed by way of compensation.

An added feature of patients born the "wrong" sex is their compulsive sexual phantasies and, frequently, their repetitive sexual habits. Sadistic behaviour towards women, for instance, is quite common; I see this behaviour as stemming from a frantic drive to try *to force* a loving response from the woman who represents mother. Though ostensibly genital, I regard this behaviour as predominantly pre-genital, and in the main as a survival response to counter the parents' narcissistically motivated rejection. Compulsive sexual phantasies, likewise, can be seen as an unsuccessful endeavour at reversing the deprivation resulting from never-experienced primary fusion-states with mother. If the compulsive sexual phantasies have a sadistic content, on the other hand, they can represent futile attempts at dissolving fusion-states that have continued into adulthood. In either case, there is an attempt by the psyche to repair damage.

Promiscuity is another ostensibly genital disguise for an oral craving, arising from a yearning to fill the void within. Alcohol or drug addiction is equally commonplace in these patients, an undisguised attempt to satisfy oral craving by oral ingestion. Eating disorders belong here too, and I have written about them elsewhere (Seligman, 1976). Homosexual phantasies and their acting-out need a mention in this context; they can be seen as an expression of the longing for the father's love and support. The patients' histories have revealed that the father, in an attempt to protect himself from his wife's pathology, opts out of the father's role, sacrificing the child in the process. He abandons the child to the mother's pathology. The child then becomes little more than the agent of his mother's narcissistic needs and ambitions. Empty and deprived, a potentially authentic personality is eroded; the child becomes an appendage to his parents.

These phenomena have become encapsulated because of the rigid inflexibility of the system. The child will wall himself in because he feels he is being constantly penetrated by his parents' ruthless wish for him to be of the "other" sex. He becomes the secretive adult. In his analysis, he tends only to risk revealing himself through his phantasies and his dreams. I have found that dream analysis becomes the predominant therapeutic exchange. It may be impossible for the analyst to help the patient overcome his terror of being, yet once again, miscast and misunderstood—the very factors which would represent a perpetuation of that permanent fear of a total dissolution of his personality which has been undermining him throughout his life.

Kohut (1977) has expressed a similar theme as follows: "The specific pathogenic personality of the parents and specific patho-genic features of the atmosphere in which the child grows up account for the maldevelopments, fixations, and unresolvable inner conflicts characterizing the adult personality". He further attributes the adult patient's disorder to

> the absence of the parents' empathic response to their child's need to be mirrored, and to find a target for his idealisation. . . . To estab-lish a dynamic connexion between these genetic factors and the specific distortions of the patient's personality most frequently constitute the principal therapeutic task of analysis. [Kohut, 1977]

Kohut implies that there is a task that analysis can fulfil, and I agree that, in spite of the degree of early and subsequent psychic damage, most patients can, up to a point, be helped by analysis to live more creative lives. Kohut has noted the painful periods of stagnation referred to earlier, and has described them as "the lethargy of the rejected self". His collective term for these patients is "the Tragic Man". In all of my own cases that belong to this cate-gory, empathic response encountered in adult life cannot make up for the traumatic failures in childhood. For patients of the "wrong" sex, with the exceptions of Mr A and of one other patient also currently in analysis with me, insurmountable obstacles to the achievement of a good enough state of integration have remained. As already described, the depressed and lonely child becomes a joyless adult, plagued by disintegration anxieties. The analyst is unlikely to succeed in substituting for the patient's faulty basic structures, but may, nevertheless, make contact with some cohesive centre within. It is surely worthwhile supporting a crumbling, frag-mented personality, and this can be most effectively achieved by a joint exploration of the events that triggered off the trouble. Thus, the remaining cohesion-producing potential is utilized as fully as possible; the patient's reasoning powers, which have remained most intact, are mobilized, and a measure of healing can take place. A sufficiently satisfactory outcome of such an analysis may then come about through the rehabilitation of compensatory structures. The analytic task may reach a termination point when the patient's self-image has become more acceptable to him and firmer. By the time adulthood is reached, the parents' inability to accept their child as he is has become internalized; their dissatisfactions have become his own. It is now he who cannot become reconciled to his gender, to the shape of his body.

I shall end this section with a reference to analytic technique. It is now my experience that the more traditional tool of interpreting the transference tends not to work with this group of patients. Transference interpretations are certainly resisted, but are also unproductive. Resistance is to be expected in all analytic work, but in this instance it cannot be interpreted usefully because of the acuteness of the underlying disintegration anxieties and the severe threat of a re-exposure of the devastating injuries of childhood. A therapeutic alliance in the usual sense is seldom, if ever, established, which is a frustrating and disheartening experience for the analyst. I suppose the patient has become too conditioned to fragmentation enfeeblement, devastation, and despair. He imposes a wall to avoid being penetrated by interpretations, though he can allow reconstruction and linking interventions from the analyst. Only thus does the analyst come at all close to becoming the patient's auxiliary personality. It can be said that some measure of shift and growth is engendered, while the basic injuries remain.

Mr A

I now come to the final section, in which I hope to show that some of the hurdles that had seemed insurmountable can be overcome. Here I am concerned with the analytic process of Mr A, a patient who was born as a replacement for a late miscarriage of a female foetus. The following words and accompanying music from Handel's "Messiah" closely echo his childhood experience: "He was despised and rejected . . . a man of sorrows, and acquainted with grief. Thy rebuke hath broken his heart . . . Neither found he any to comfort him . . . He was cut off out of the land of the living".

These words may sound extravagant; nevertheless, they poignantly describe a childhood devoid of any spark of affection from either parent. Mr A was, and to some extent still is, the inconsolable son of disappointed, frustrated parents whom he could not appease, however hard he had tried. His realization that he had been born the wrong person of the wrong sex was distilled out of personal memories, and also a series of early dreams, all concerned with members of the Royal Family, and his endeavour to gain entry into their elect orbit by countless attempts to ingratiate himself with them.

He was still in analysis, grappling with the inheritance of an irreversible sense of worthlessness and the problem engendered by his bisexual leaning—a failed attempt at an acceptable compromise.

At this point I will quote a short extract from Jung's *Tavistock Lectures*: "The body is a most doubtful friend, because it produces things we do not like. . . . Sometimes it forms the skeleton in the cupboard. Nevertheless, there is more to man than his biological roots, important as they are—it is the search for the self that remains the ultimate goal" (Jung, 1935).

To convey to a suffering individual some notion of archetypal themes helps him beyond measure to accept that his conflicts are not his personal failure only, but that they also link him with human destiny at large. Furthermore, Jung's idea that dreams and symbols have a compensatory function, and are a natural reaction of the self-regulation of the psychic system, can be an invaluable aid when despair and stagnation set in.

In Mr A's case, his analysis has been characterized by the emergence of a number of crucially important dreams and symbols in a way that I have seldom before experienced. This has made his analysis one of unique interest and satisfaction, and he is becoming an individuated man in spite of his debilitating personal history.

I have already referred to some of Mr A's early history, in that he was born as a replacement for a female child that was miscarried. He was the first-born live son of an orthodox Jewish couple, and the eldest son in this particular culture carries something of a "divine" significance. He was blond, blue-eyed, and seen as "perfect", a show-off boost to his narcissistic parents. His own personal identity was not perceived by them; they saddled him with the archetypal image of a divine being, Jung's "Divine Child" and something of a Lucifer, an angelic bringer of light. His parents were quite exceptionally unconscious people, thus swamping him with archetypal images that were not mediated by any human or personal relatedness. He was dressed all in white, with kid gloves, and it became imperative to his parents that he kept himself quite immaculately white and spotless.

As you might expect, the only avenue open to his tender ego against its total obliteration was by a precipitous development of self-reliance and autonomy, and an early identification of himself with the "Healer" archetype. The symbolic death of both parents that, Jung tells us, is the prerequisite to the beginning of the individuation process, already occurred for Mr A at the age of four when he more or less wrote them off, and became acutely aware of being "different" and "other". Nevertheless, he felt evil, worthless, and a disappointment to them, and an urge to realize his own true self was engendered; he missed out on being a child. There are parallels here with Jung's own development. It is clear that Mr A, this solitary and unusual little boy, was troubling and alienating to his conventional undifferentiated parents.

There was a further catastrophe. When Mr A had his routine school medical examination it was revealed that he was far from perfect and flawless. Quite the reverse. He was found to have a major congenital defect, and to be suffering from impaired hearing. Overnight he ceased to be for his parents, the "bringer of light", and became the "fallen angel", the Satan figure, the "devil" child. After the birth of his brother, he became the Cain, his brother the Abel.

Both Jung (1942) and Rivkah Scharf (1967) have written extensively on the Satan theme, Satan being seen as God's first child who fell from grace and ceased to be a divine angel, becoming the "Adversary". He led a degraded, shadow-like existence at the side of Yahweh—he was the "enemy". Similarly, Mr A became the personification of his parent's shadows. In Scharf's thesis on 'The figure of Satan in the Old Testament', she writes as follows:

> The adversary is, at the same time, the course of individual consciousness. . . . Psychologically, Satan is the stronger . . . and in the Book of Job has the function of a messenger . . . Satan is the destructive doubt in the divine personality . . . whilst Yahweh prefers to avert his own demonic nature. . . . He is also God's destructive activity, which has its origin in God's doubt regarding

man. . . . Satan appears as a disturbance. . . . Satan is here truly
Lucifer, bringing man the knowledge of God, but through the
suffering he inflicts upon him. . . . Satan is the misery of the world,
through which alone man is driven inwards. It is Satan who drives
man beyond himself, out of the paradise of animal-like existence
. . . Satan, as the dark side of God, together with the angel, the light
side, are two aspects of God fighting over man. . . . Satan, as the
antagonist of the Messiah, is the bringer of death to the world.
[Scharf, 1967]

Jung, in "Psychology and religion" (1962), expressed parallel
views. He sees significance. He was blond, blue-eyed, and seen as
"perfect", a show-off boost to his narcissistic Satan, the adversary,
as "the other man in me", and described Christ and the devil as
"equal and opposite", and calling the Lucifer legend "a 'therapeutic' myth". There follows some significant sentences, which I should
like to quote: "Life being an energic process, needs the opposites,
for without opposition, there is no energy. Good and evil are simply
the moral aspects of this natural polarity. . . . One of the toughest
roots of all evil is unconsciousness" (Jung, 1962, p. 197). In other
words Satan is the elder, Christ the younger Son of God.

This takes us back to Mr A, who, as I have described, had been
Lucifer, the angel who had fallen from the heavenly and earthly
hierarchy and was disowned and rejected by his parents. When his
brother was born, it was he who displaced Mr A as the divine
Lucifer child who could do no wrong in his parents' eyes, in spite
of his becoming a scoundrel, handsome and degenerate, the
mother's gigolo whom she bailed out of every scrape he got himself
into throughout his adult life.

In reminding you of what I said in the earlier part of this paper,
regarding that seemingly irreducible complex that remains when
someone is born of the "wrong" sex, I gave some examples and
observations that indicated that such patients often retain a hermaphroditic appearance and life-style. They are frequently bisexual,
being beset with their own sex's physical characteristics, but with a
deep longing to be of the other sex and thus gain, at last, the
parents' love. Jung has pointed out that the hermaphrodite is the
archetypal subduer of intolerable conflicts. Mr A, too, was bisexual
when we first met, married with children, but nevertheless somewhat effeminate in his gait and posture, and with homosexual

leanings. Before long, his dreams began to reveal an over-development of his feminine characteristics, an unconscious manoeuvre to ingratiate himself with his mother, Gradually, a more comfortable alliance between his masculine and feminine sides developed, the one becoming the vehicle for the other. He had a decisive dream that confirmed him in his manhood, and that made on Mr A an impact similar to the one that the dream about the enormous phallus had on Jung's life. Mr A's transference to me also shifted, and I began to stand in for his always "missing" father, who had died some years previously.

I should like to relate this dream, as well as two of the most significant subsequent ones. It went as follows:

> Mr A was in a boat with an older man, who asked him to look down into the deep water and he would see a tower, Mr A did so, and the light at the top of the tower was fifty feet below him (like the eye on the gigantic phallus in Jung's dream). The man encouraged him to really *look,* and Mr A became aware of the awe-inspiring depth of the water. He was riveted to what he saw. He could see the base of the tower on the seabed, with its cables and tubes. He saw the total structure with all its intricacies. When their boat came ashore, some milk bottles that stood in their path were removed. (I took those to be symbols of his mother-fixation and his feminine identification.)

> Next day, Mr A wrote me a note that simply said, "Thank you for the gift of my tower". In the next session Mr A recalled how, as a boy, he had visited Paris with a school party; the other children went up the Eiffel Tower while he searched the shops for his mother's favourite perfume.

I cannot here enter into the detail of the inordinate amount of work that has continued in Mr A's analysis, but there are two more of his dreams, which will, I think, confirm that his individuation process is well on the way. Both dreams occurred during the course of one year, separated by an interval of about three months.

The first of these was, in my view, a symbolic death and rebirth, and Mr A called it "transformation by fire". The dream went as follows:

> I am in a coffin in order to be cremated. My coffin is placed in a big building, which is simultaneously a crematorium, a dance hall, a wedding parlour, and an entertainment centre. All of life was enacted

there. There were parts of bodies there, and a man demonstrating organ-replacement surgery. But I was intended for the transforming fire. I took off all my valuables, I placed them in a pile, consisting of all the objects I carry but that are not me—my ring, keys, glasses, and teeth. I was naked in the coffin, just myself, without my worldly possessions. I realized I would only be remembered in people's hearts, by those to whom I am important.

We now come to the last dream that I wish to mention. Mr A was crossing the road in order to meet his spiritual leader. Though still quite young, he had a long beard and was in a wheelchair. The reason was that he had something wrong with his right foot; it was partially paralysed. Mr A and the man then shook hands, but the man was unable to speak, and had an expression of suffering and great wisdom. Mr A was affected by the man's depth of personality, felt strongly drawn to him, and put a pillow underneath his ailing foot to protect it and felt fortified by this encounter in spite of the man's frail appearance. Soon the man ceased to be paralysed, and he began gently to stroke Mr A's head and neck.

This dream heralded Mr A's discovery of the "wise old man" within himself, whereas previously he had met him only in others, including a dream in which he had a memorable meeting with Jung. Jung himself tells of a life-sustaining dialogue with an inner figure (who also appears in Goethe's *Faust*) whom he named Philemon. He emerged following Jung's traumatic break with Freud, which had engendered an acute crisis in his psychic equilibrium. Philemon, too, had a lame foot, and a winged spirit, a free "other than himself" personality, and was like a compensatory element to the inner chaos threatening Jung at that time (Jung, 1935).

Mr A is still only in mid-life, and the injured foot of his "wise man" may symbolize his own wounds, which will never quite heal.

An awareness of the personal tragedies that have concerned us here is a timely reminder that life cannot be severed from its biological roots. Years ago, I found a quotation from Sakya Muni, which has long stayed with me. It goes as follows: "Whosoever discovers that grief comes from unrequited love will retire into the jungle and there remain". People who go into analysis are looking for a way out of the jungle, though for some, a refractory element will remain. Fortunately, however, there are rare exceptions when a resolution is achieved in spite of major obstacles.

Summary

This chapter attempts to explore some root causes of prolonged periods of stagnation in those analyses that initially seemed to go well, but subsequently became bogged down. My earlier ideas that the cause was the symbiotic entanglement with one parent to the exclusion of the other, who would need to be reclaimed before wholeness could be achieved, had proved no longer adequate, An evaluation of my more recent work revealed an ultimately refractory element consisting of an irremediable encapsulated affliction, which I have specified as that of the patient having been born of the "wrong" sex. This calamity is further compounded by the parents' narcissistic illness, which effectively prevents them from becoming reconciled to their "wrong" child. The child continues, without success, to seek the parents' approval, remaining merely the agent of their narcissistic needs, their appendage. He is trapped in a permanent fusion with them, or else he becomes walled off. His sense of autonomy withers, hence the long periods of stagnation in these analyses. I set out to formulate how a partially satisfactory outcome may be brought about through the rehabilitation of compensatory structures. In most of these cases a measure of shift and growth is engendered, while basic injuries remain. Nevertheless, in exceptional cases, like that of Mr. A, which is taken up in the final section, I set out to show that seemingly insurmountable obstacles can be overcome.

CHAPTER NINE

On death and survival

"For he who lives more lives than one
More deaths than one must die"

(Oscar Wilde)

Our closest encounters from before birth mould our lives and prescribe the interplay between our individuality and its manifestation. Each confrontation with death is intricately interwoven with a complex web of significant personal relationships that are interdependent and ceaselessly impinge one on the other.

This should be constantly kept in mind when confronted with a person in crisis. Though he may strike us as a solitary bundle of distress, he is nevertheless compounded of a maze of interacting phenomena spanning the generations, endlessly entangled.

Having reiterated the obvious, which can nevertheless be overlooked, I should like to turn to the predicament of the bereaved, which may be twofold. He may remain the victim of an irredeemable loss, or he may emerge from darkness into dawn and become the survivor. In my view, this is a very vital distinction.

We live at a time when we are never allowed to forget the instant menace of violence, destruction, and death on a vast scale, death from without, but also from within. We live in the shadow of the atom bomb. The young, most especially, see death, premature extinction, as a certainty. A host of nuclear missiles are close to their own back yards. Thus it has come about, as I see it, that the survivor is emerging as the prospective carrier of life and hope. It is no longer the tragic hero, the martyr who has sacrificed his life, though he may inspire pity and awe, but the figure of the survivor who is now a saviour symbol in our society.

All men are in a sense victims, and vulnerability is a painful condition of existence, therefore our culture and its media have elected to provide distraction aimed at displacing our awareness of just that which is the most terrible for the individual to bear, the death of those closest to him as well as the prospect of his own death. Yet, in the imagination, both are ever with us; even the moment of birth can be the first experience of a sudden lunge into a void.

So we are all of us not only victims of our vulnerability, but also potential survivors who, at the moment of crisis are in urgent need of finding within ourselves that vital factor which takes us beyond despair to the point of willing to survive, requiring a capacity to endure pain and guilt, an unshakeable faith in the value of life. To become a survivor is to transcend an experience of death in life.

We have all of us observed how the personal experience of death reduces human capacity, can dissolve the personality, and cause collapse. Death remains an aspect of our existence that man is unable to alter fundamentally or to overcome, but if it overwhelms him he is its victim. What then enables the will to carry on in the face of the traumatic loss of unity with a loved one? Surely, a phase of profound mourning is endurable if the numbed desire for living can only thus be restored. Otherwise, a sense of awful helplessness continues, a state that can become so acute as to threaten the life of the afflicted person, if not in body, certainly in spirit. The ultimate challenge is to keep sufficiently intact as a person so as to be open to resurgence and to the emotional support that others may then have to offer.

It is at this juncture that the struggle to survive and the struggle to remain human becomes one. To hold on, to wait, to stand back, and to allow time to pass is the survivor's primary need. Only thus will he perhaps prevent remaining a victim, a falling back into random death, a spiritual vacuum, a persistent anguish and empty time. When the event of death shatters the rhythm of ongoing life, the will of the spirit and the will of the body must join in common cause.

Once the bereaved person has survived the first, the most desperate phase, he may often, with the help and support of understanding people, discover the values and capacities that he did not know of in himself. Having passed in pain beyond the personal loss, he may find himself face to face and in peace with the numinous power of life. This is the religious, the transcendent dimension of the survivor's experience, the unexpected, invaluable return from oblivion.

The Ship of Death

I

And it is time to go, to bid farewell
To one's own self

V

Build then the ship of death, for you must take
the longest journey, to oblivion.

And die the death, the long and painful death
that lies between the old self and the new . . .

Already the dark and endless ocean of the end
is washing in through the breaches of our wounds;
already the flood is upon us.

VII

Launch out the fragile soul
in the fragile ship of courage, the ark of faith

There is no port, there is nowhere to go
only the deepening blackness darkening still

IX

And yet out of eternity a thread
separates itself on the blackness

Ah wait, wait, for there's the dawn,
the cruel dawn of coming back to life
out of oblivion.

Oh build your ship of death. Oh build it!
for you will need it . . . [Lawrence, 1933, *Selected Poems*]

Surviving a beloved person can become, at least for some, a time of growth, and of becoming more fully human. The way down is also the way up. The passage through loss and suffering may come to constitute greater self-knowledge, an intensification of spiritual fulfilment and authentic selfhood. Not only inner resources, but also past and present relationships are quite decisive here.

Even so, the pain is always present, in the body, and in the heart and in the soul. It is at this point that life meets death as an equal. Death will not retreat; to come to terms with it is to live beyond fear and despair. Though solitude remains the ultimate anguish, some of it will dissolve. The survivor, who at first feels he has lost everything except his own small life, may come to incorporate some of the qualities of the deceased into his own being and from there go on to discover some new values for himself.

Nevertheless, there are many who are overwhelmed by a loss that has deprived them of any sense of identity, who feel quite empty at their centre and depersonalized. To be faced with the total destruction of both the "I" and the "Thou" is the most devastating bereavement of all. At the heart of being there is only a dull, empty silence. A healing, loving bond with another, or others, will be crucial, and may become the opportunity for unborn elements of the self to be born, perhaps even for the first time, so that a new arena of capacity for living and for relatedness may then be opened up. The ability to relate is, after all, the key to the quality of life from the cradle to the grave. Therein lies the hope, and the future.

CHAPTER TEN

"Experts in mothercraft"

Mary Crotty's "Communication to the Editors" in the final issue of *The British Journal of Psychiatric Social Work* has given me a welcome opportunity to make some further comments on the controversial topics she has raised.

She discusses the concept of the "good mother" and she also speaks of the function of the "expert in mothercraft". This has led me to consider some of the many roles played by the numerous experts who commonly influence the life of mother and child. I suppose most of us would agree that a "good" mother needs to be sufficiently at one with herself to resist the temptation of moulding her child to some pattern unconsciously necessary to her. Hence a "good" mother will not be likely to stifle the child by applying to him preconceived axioms of upbringing and routine which are not appropriate to him. I agree, then, that this implies the opposite of a rigid set of universally applicable rules such as Mary Crotty deplores in some child-guidance work. On the contrary, the small, intense, but ever-widening world of mother and child should be individual and unique to them.

This undoubtedly makes a great demand on the mother, for not only should she be able to cope with her own inner difficulties and conflicts in order not to weigh down her offspring with them, but also she must have confidence in herself as a mother. And this is by no means easy. It requires a deep conviction that she is inherently well equipped for motherhood, that somewhere she, and only she, knows best what is right for her child.

Where, then, do the "experts in mothercraft" come in? From the point of view of mental health, these experts seem to be of two kinds. First, there are those who can function only by imposing their expertness on the mother's apparent inexpertness so that, in spite of their knowledge and skill, they very often inhibit her ability to make use of her natural endowment. For instance: an "expert" sister in the maternity ward who impresses on the very new mother only just beginning to emerge from a most tumultuous experience that she is a hopeless failure if she cannot immediately establish successful breast-feeding. Or the neighbours, mothers and mothers-in-law, who seem always to think that the baby is not warm enough, is underfed or cries because the mother is neglecting him or is "too modern". There are those workers at infant welfare clinics who have discouraged many a mother by telling her, somewhat high-handedly, "It is time you took some of *our* advice for a change." And what about the "placid" expert children's nurse who, more often than not, succeeds in turning out ostensibly "placid" children? How has she achieved this result, frequently welcome to the mother who employs her? And what boiling cauldrons of hate, resentment, despair, and longing may be hidden under a child's calm exterior?

But there is another kind of expert, perhaps something of an ideal, always sought but not yet found. It is to him that the mother turns when she or her child, mostly both, have become over-whelmed by their own and each other's difficulties. Somewhere the germ of a full and happy mother–child relationship is buried and may need much skilled care and support before it can grow strong enough to remain intact throughout the ups and downs of growth and upbringing. This expert, then, if successful, will have helped to establish the inner and outer conditions that are necessary to the fulfilment of all potentialities within this individual and unique small world of mother and child referred to earlier. Here, then, lies the scope of child-guidance workers (no less than on nurses and all others engaged in the welfare of mother and child) as against the other kind of "experts in mothercraft". The latter impart some of their expert skill, but at the same time are liable to undermine the mother's own inherent expertness to deal with her child; while the former help to awaken and to restore it.

I am now turning to Mary Crotty's point that women who are psychiatric social workers, or have followed other professions, and who have "imagination, perception and intelligence rather than placidity" are less likely to be good at "baby minding". This seems to imply that these qualities are not only wasted, but even out of place in the intimate day-to-day contact with little children, whereas I believe that hardly anywhere are these gifts more needed and arouse greater response than just here. I also feel that if the Mental Health Course has given us, as surely it should, something of a greater insight into ourselves and thereby into other people, it has also, quite incidentally, helped to make us better mothers.

This leads me to my last point: Mary Crotty's implication that the "management of bibs and potties", the problem of temper tantrums, food fads, and outbursts of aggression can be better coped with by the "placid expert in mothercraft" than by the mother herself, or, alternatively, that these problems are definitely inferior and less deserving of her preoccupation than her professional calling. Of course, everyone must find her own solution to this most difficult of problems, but, as anyone with experience of little children knows, all tasks connected with the physical functions can least of all be executed by another person. For it is just the food, the potty, the bath, the bib that are in the focus of a child's emotional life and therefore have a vital bearing on all his future relationships. It is here that his loves, hates, and passions first express themselves; and unless they find response in a predominantly loving and accepting mother, how is a child to deal with his feelings and learn to come to satisfactory terms with the "realities" of life?

Book reviews

Neumann, Erich. *Kunst und Schöpferisches Unbewusstes* (*Art and the Creative Unconscious*). 1980. Pp. vii + 166. Zurich: Daimon Verlag, pbk.

This volume, first published by Rascher in 1954, contains three essays concerned with the relationship of the artist to society. Neumann postulates that it is the artist's task to give expression to the original, formless archetypal patterns. The resultant images are, in his view, influenced by the era, by society, and by the context in which they are conceived, while, at all times, taking on their own individual mould from the psyche of the creative artist. The task of the artist, therefore, is to create by means of his own imagination, rather than be dominated by prevailing norms and the culture of the time in which he lives.

The three essays are headed: "Leonardo da Vinci and the mother archetype", "Art and its epoch", and "Comments regarding Marc Chagall".

In his essay on Leonardo da Vinci, the author concentrates on the connection between the creative artist and his work, combined with the influence of the collective unconscious, most particularly the archetype of the great mother. This leads him beyond the point where Freud made his stand. Furthermore, a clarification of how Leonardo's creative genius was predominantly affected by those very core problems that eventually became the collective unconscious of modern man.

The fundamental connection between the creative individual to his epoch and the central tenor of the current climate in which he lives, which find their expression in modern art—these are the themes of the two remaining essays. Through an understanding of modern art and its creative representatives, it is stated, we clarify our interpretation of the current cultural setting, and in addition, we gain insight into the overall psychic dilemma of modern man.

The creative person is said to be the most profound representative of his time, or else his unconscious may throw up the very content which is missing in his culture. These people come closest to the psychically ill who, just like their creative counterparts, may be affected and overwhelmed by the very influences that are the most crucial for the future development of mankind. It is in this sense that modern art is equally enlightening to the understanding of contemporary health as it is to those that have become ill. Moreover, psychic contents that emerge during the healing and individuation process, together with the creative material of man are vital factors in the understanding of modern art.

At the centre of these processes we find the creative source of the psyche which, in art just as much as in religion, fosters the development of the masculine consciousness and its opposite, the feminine, which influence countless variations and ever-new routes to an individual's life, and the overall culture of mankind.

*Social Casework in Marital Problems:
The Development of a Psychodynamic Approach.* By a group of caseworkers at the Family Discussion Bureau. 1955. Pp. xii + 199. London: Tavistock Publications.

The effects of an unhappy or disrupted marriage make themselves felt, directly or indirectly, in every branch of social work. Family caseworkers are constantly being confronted with some of its many repercussions. For this reason alone a book describing a new approach to casework with marital problems is long overdue and is indeed welcome. This stimulating, lucidly written study represents something of a perfect marriage between scientific detachment and deepening insight into human motivation.

As most of the readers of this volume probably know, the Family Discussion Bureau was set up in 1948 by the Family Welfare Association, and this report represents a study of their first five years' experience. It begins with a description of the development of the Bureau, followed by a full account of the organization and training of the team of workers and an outline of the psychological theory on which their work is based. There is also a detailed account of their casework methods, illustrated by a considerable number of actual cases. The last part of the book deals with the use of case conferences and assesses casework results. There is also a discussion of the Bureau's relations to other social institutions and, finally, an estimation of its potential value and significance.

We are thus enabled to follow a new social casework venture through from its first inception to its firm establishment, for it seems most likely that the Bureau, in one form or another, has come to stay. Throughout the book, the experimental and exploratory character of the work is stressed; there is nothing final in their procedure, except that the standards of training and the actual organization of the casework are laid down. Viewpoints and experiences are pooled in regular joint case conferences in which a consultant psychoanalyst takes part. Thus, the workers spare themselves some of the tribulations that social work in isolation is apt to involve. They are able to discuss their difficulties, and the cases are greatly helped in their development by the contribution of others who are not directly involved.

The book raises certain interesting questions, such as whether there is something in the marriage relationship that lends itself most particularly to a psychodynamic approach, or whether the therapeutic skill that the team has developed might also be applicable in other branches of social work. A closely related method is, in fact, being practised by many psychiatric social workers in Child Guidance Clinics. On the other hand, some of us may ask, as do the authors, whether a different approach to marital difficulties, based for instance on an educational and preventive standpoint or on a more directive and practical one, would not also be effective. Dr Sutherland himself says in his introduction to the book, "It need hardly be said that it is unlikely that the work of the Bureau is the only answer to the marriage in difficulties." But it has certainly been successful in many cases. No doubt, one of the reasons is that the psychodynamic approach takes account of the importance of childhood and adolescence relationships to consequent marriage problems. The marital relationship "involves the personality at deepest levels and is itself a vital primary relationship, where an unconscious 'transference' of expectations, demands, impulses, and anxieties that were features of the earlier relationships is inevitably both more readily and more fully made." Thus the equilibrium of two marriage partners can be easily disturbed, setting into motion a pattern of more primitive, often infantile reactions that quickly chase away the loving feelings and positive forces that brought the couple together in the first place. High hopes soon give way to a feeling of being the helpless victim of irrevocable circumstances, and a complete break seems the only way out. The sheer weight of all this is likely to produce an effect of despair not only on the client but also on the caseworker, who may feel baffled and lost. It is therefore fortunate that the Bureau's team bring to their intricate task a fair measure of insight into their own emotional responses. Caseworkers are, of course, carefully selected and go through a probationary period and two years of supervised training. Husbands and wives frequently both come to the Bureau but are seen by different workers and not, as a rule, together. Not all cases that present themselves are accepted; those that are may have anything from one to seventy-five interviews. According to the statistics supplied, forty-two out of 100 cases during a period of twenty months showed "marked" or "considerable" improvement, for thirty "some" progress was recorded, while the remaining twenty-eight did not appear to improve.

Although a tentative evaluation of casework results is included in the book it would nevertheless be welcome if the Bureau would concentrate some of its further researches on an even more detailed analysis of the type of case they are best able to help with the tools they have developed, and also on an analysis of the cases that were abandoned. They have gone some way in this direction by establishing that the longer cases were, on the whole, much more successful than the short-term ones. The authors frequently stress the wider implications of a deteriorating or of an improving marriage relationship, especially on the children as well as on the physical health of all the family and the clients' achievements at work. Already in the introductory chapter they point out that "for the Family Discussion Bureau, the unit was not for the individual but the marriage, and behind it the family; and this meant a significantly different outlook from that of the analyst who must be concerned exclusively with the individual who is his patient". Yet their technique demands that they concentrate on the emotional problems of husbands and wives, and they agree that it is difficult for them to assess the broader repercussions of their work. As the authors suggest, this, too, coupled with a follow-up study of cases, would seem to be a fruitful field for further investigation, Readers will welcome the many detailed case reports that afford good insight into the problems with which the Bureau have to deal and into the application of their methods.

The reporting of these cases must itself have been a problem because of the confidential nature of the interviews, which has made it necessary to omit many of the unique aspects of each marriage. Perhaps this is the reason why certain stereotyped emotional patterns seem to repeat themselves in practically all cases and the impression is created that the marriage partners who come to the Bureau are the victims of identical psychological mechanisms. A related difficulty is how to convey to the reader the emotional atmosphere of the interviews so as to reproduce faithfully the effect on the client of the worker's psychological interpretations. Some of these appear to be abrupt and almost theoretical when reported, while in fact they probably were appropriate and helpful.

Though some of the readers of this present volume may have difficulties in accepting the Freudian theories on which the Bureau's approach is based, it is certain that intense casework of this kind cannot be undertaken without the knowledge and conviction that unconscious forces and irrational attitudes create most of the conflicts in human relationships. It would be a most welcome response to this important book if it would encourage the formation of further similar groups.

Two publications: Lawrence, Marilyn, *The Anorexic Experience*. 1984. Pp. 142. The Women's Press, pbk; Spignesi, Angelyn, *Starving Women: A psychology of Anorexia Nervosa.* 1985. Pp. 158. Spring Publications, pbk.

Eating disorders have become all too commonplace. They have taken on epidemic proportions. A spate of books on the subject is therefore to be expected.

It was with some trepidation that I agreed to review yet another two which, nevertheless, provided an unexpected bonus. At long last, both opened the way to a shift from the exclusively personal and family approach to anorexia nervosa. The two authors, each in her own way, recognize the relevance of the transpersonal, of collective forces on the aetiology of this illness, while approaching the subject quite differently. For this reason alone, and for the clarity, brevity, and compactness of the books, they are to be welcomed.

Though anorexia and its counterpart, bulimia, are, in their acute form, unquestionably pathological conditions, originating in disturbed interpersonal and family relationships, these alone do not account for the choice of symptoms. The alarming escalation of these illnesses has, in my view, made it imperative to acknowledge those transpersonal, sociological aspects of our era that unquestionably influence eating behaviour in particular. Are analytical psychologists prone to pay too little heed to collective aspects of psychic states to which Jung repeatedly drew our attention long ago?

Marilyn Lawrence opens up this avenue in her introduction but does not pursue it. Instead she develops a feminist line with which I find myself out of sympathy, the more so as I have treated a number of male anorexic patients. She does, however, recognize in a novel and illuminating book rich in clinical material that anorexia is a condition that is rife in the affluent West, in the so-called "developed", opulent parts of the world. Let me add that other members of the human race so aptly known as the "third" world are starving to death in their millions.

How can such a state of affairs do other than engender transpersonal guilt and conflict repressed and denied by most, but

manifesting itself in primitive disturbances such as eating disorders, which are always accompanied by depression and guilt, the
more so if reinforced by the unrecognized guilt and hunger for love
originating in early parental relationships, most especially with the
mother.

Angelyn Spignesi's book, unlike Marilyn Lawrence's, is not
clinical in its approach. She develops a wholly different, collective
investigation into the causation of anorexia. She does so explicitly
and thoroughly, with scholarly insight and some feminist bias. She
concentrates on the symbolic dimension of the affliction, exploring
anorexia through imagery. She favours the archetypal and mytho-
logical aspect. She does it very well. She is preoccupied with the
woman starving for nourishment from the underworld from which,
she asserts, she has been cut off for centuries.

I am less at home with her book than that of Marilyn Lawrence,
which in no way detracts from its high standard. Her approach
simply conflicts with my experience that serious disorders that are
difficult to treat and involve grave risks demand a predominantly
clinical approach together with careful transference work.

Angelyn Spignesi makes one particularly interesting point at
the outset of her book: "Anorexia is the modern offspring of hysteria". On reflection, I have come to follow her thinking. It could be
something like this. The hysteric's compulsive preoccupation with,
and fear of, hunger for sex is replaced in the anorexic and the
bulimic person by both fear of eating and a compulsive preoccupation with food and an insatiable hunger for it, or for what it represents. These patients are taken over by a total absorption with
weight and dieting, manifesting itself by a never-ending coercive
and manipulative struggle with the environment. Perhaps this
comparison makes anorexia not so much an offspring as perhaps a
twin sister of hysteria? The reader will have to decide. Whichever
is the case, both hysteria and anorexia are apt specific symptom-
choices for the more fragile members of symbiotic-type families
that are plagued with a fear of annihilation.

Both books are attractive, eminently readable and well written.
Marilyn Lawrence's, being the less sophisticated, the more direct
and explicit, is certainly a useful introduction to the topic. Angelyn
Spignesi's is the more challenging.

Rode, C. H. *Zur Phänomenologie der Magrsucht. Eine tiefenpsychologische Fallstudie zur Psychosomatik.* 1979. Zürich, *Psychosomatische Medizin,* 8(3), pp. 109. (*The Aetiology of Anorexia Nervosa—a Case Study in Depth of the Psychosomatic Factors.*)

This issue of the Swiss *Journal of Psychosomatic Medicine* is exclusively devoted to a detailed study of a case of anorexia nervosa. In a stimulating, erudite article the author casts his net wide. He conducts his readers through the tangled web of the aetiology of the illness, and through the treatment period of almost three years. He is alive to the dynamics of the transference–countertransference manifestations and puts to good use his patient's fertile symbolic material, her dreams, paintings, and stories. The reader is provided with a rich feast.

Rode is much taken up with Jung's ideas of the self regulating system in the psyche, perhaps not acknowledging sufficiently how chaotic this system becomes in psychotic states. His grasp, however, of the psychosomatic mechanisms in anorexics is comprehensive, and these are discussed with admirable clarity.

Furthermore, relevant psychological theories from the Jungian spectrum of the literature are extensively referred to. Yet, by confining himself to Jungian contributions, the author inevitably omits many important references.

Rode's account shows exceptional willingness to reveal himself and his analytic style, his objective as well as his subjective experiences. He does not confine himself to his patient's struggles; he also dwells on his own. He reveals his considerable skills as a clinician, and demonstrates his ability to formulate and organize the material. Dr A Hicklin's editorial comments emphasize that in psychosomatic disorders, and most especially in cases of anorexia nervosa, the outer and inner worlds are inextricably interwoven. Non-verbal communications take on a unique significance. He stresses that anorexics almost totally negate life so that the ever-threatening, potentially avoidable confrontation with death, the final catastrophe, overshadows the work. A sense of foreboding and guilt are never absent. The therapist is constantly pushed to his limit.

Rode expands these themes, and sees these patients as suffering from "a dent in the lifeline" that culminates in their illness, the last sequence in the process that represents an attempt at achieving total autonomous control of all body processes. This endeavour, pathological though it is, constitutes a striving to undo the basic fault in the mother–child relationship. He regards the illness as a stubborn attempt at magically overcoming all that stands for mother by vomiting her out. The patient hopes that she will simultaneously demolish all her longing for the idealized good mother whom she has despaired of ever encountering. Thus the omnipotent baby takes control of the adult, a doomed attempt at a recovery by way of regression.

Rode refers to this sequence as a "form of animus possession" aimed at the achievement of total victory over the reverses of life. I can only partially accept this formulation: the giving up of the omnipotent baby is a major wrench, the more so when the mother–imago is entirely negatively tinged; ultimate liberation from her would appear to be achievable only through her or the patient's death.

In a well-written account, Rode highlights other significant pathological elements in anorexia. The negation of sexuality, instinctual drives and materialism for instance; that is, all areas of the mother principle, a compensation affected by a seemingly total dedication to spirituality. This is the rebellion of the all too earth-bound ravenous mother. Anorexia is further described as "a game of death with chess", because the personal mother experience has become a confrontation with the archetypal dragon monster. The patient continues to remain oblivious of the threatening reality of her own death. All persecutory anxiety is diverted into the terrible mother. Only in a total overcoming of her would her insatiable propensities be appeased. The patient would have triumphed.

As to the patient's own devouring traits, these are seen by the author as manifestations of her murderous animus. In the therapy, he aims to help her towards a separation from it. Only then, he postulates, can her own libido be freed and become available for the enhancement of her life.

I was left wondering whether this objective is too limited and might shed light on the partially inconclusive outcome.

The specifically Jungian slant makes Rode's article especially welcome to the readers of the Journal. His quote "every psychotherapist not only has his own method; he himself is that method" is borne out in his practice, and provides a moving illustration of Jung's contention that it is not only the patient, but also the therapist, who is transformed in the analytic process.

Younger colleagues in particular will appreciate Rode's vivid presentation, which clearly demonstrates how the analytic alliance becomes the facilitating environment, allowing both participants to grow. His generous acknowledgment of the fascination and the anxiety accompanied by escalating emotional tension triggered off by his patient's psychotic components is refreshing. He goes on to describe how his therapeutic libido became tinged with the archetype of the Messiah and the Healer, and how his "intellectual eros" was stimulated, a feature of working with psychotics.

At one point only does Rode refer to Freud and his notion of a "transference cure", linking it with Jung's "self regulating mechanisms of the psyche" and their potential for the repair of a damaged personality. In my view, this particular connecting is too simplistic, if not invalid.

The article is outstanding for its clarity and cohesion, without any sacrifice to the acknowledging of the grey areas of uncertainty and setbacks. The author has successfully resisted the temptation of presenting his readers with a successful outcome, so seductive when writing up a case, and a useful shield against despair.

I recommend this article, most especially to aspiring analysts, and to any reader with an interest in psychosomatic disorders. I hope that an English translation will become available in due course.

Herzog, Edgar. *Psyche and Death (Death-Demons in Folklore, Myths and Modern Dreams)*. 1983. Translated by David Cox and Eugene Rolf. Pp. 224. Dallas: Spring Publications, pbk.

This awe-inspiring book originated as a course of lectures at the C. G. Jung Institute in Zürich that were subsequently published in German by Rascher Verlag, edited by the Curatorium of the Institute. An English and American edition first appeared in 1967, published by Hodder and Stoughton and G. P. Putnam and Sons, New York, respectively.

Psyche and Death may, therefore, already be familiar to some readers. Perhaps it was more relevant when first published than it is today. The face of the world, and therefore of the collective psyche in particular, has undergone profound changes in the intervening years, especially, I think, as regards attitudes to death, and therefore to life. This statement, a generalization, reflects the author's almost exclusively collective approach to his subject of death. However universal an event the cessation of life is, it is undeniable that any direct confrontation with absolute finality has a powerful, if not devastating, impact on individuals and their personal existence.

This book lacks a balance between the personal and the collective, and I therefore found it difficult to read, sometimes alienating, and certainly remote. Furthermore, I question whether the collective psyche is fixed, rigid, and permanent. Does it not change, to some extent at least, with the times? If so, presumably its symbolic representations also alter.

Psyche and Death consists of a two-part study. The first is concerned with fairytales, folklore, and legends variously illustrating archaic death images, which originally revealed themselves in the guise of animals as wolves, horses, dogs, snakes, and birds. In the author's view, the same holds true today, and death takes similar forms, appearing to human consciousness mainly through dreams. I think this contention is open to discussion.

Part two focuses on the dreams of patients, fifty-six of them, some dreamed by the patients of other therapists, all, in my view open to an infinite variety of interpretations. Herzog links the dreams with the persons, scenes, and drama of the ancient past, and occasionally, all too rarely with the living present of the dreamers.

The depth of the research, the wealth of sources, the careful detail, are indeed impressive, and there may be many who will find a work of this stature of great value. There will be others who prefer a more contemporary, and a more clinical approach.

The author's main focus is on man's relation to, and coming to terms with, death. He postulates that a growing acceptance of death is a condition of life. "To open oneself to death is to accept the aspect of 'becoming', that is, of transformation, which is the very stuff of life." That may be a valid point of view, but not the only one. "Becoming" may not hinge only on a capacity to come to terms with death, which for some is less difficult than adjusting to living. "Becoming" and succumbing can be uncomfortably close. Many younger patients, in particular, seemingly court death, having failed to find meaning and value in their lives. I have my doubts about whether collective phenomena enable them to become reconciled to their personal tragedies and traumas. I think the opposite is more likely to be the case. For the majority of people, their own significant personal characteristics and their most important personal relationships are more likely to mediate otherwise unfathomable and overwhelming events in their lives.

In a society in which material values are increasingly stressed while millions exist in poverty or starve to death, in which man has become the victim of the menace of high-energy physics, increasingly more sophisticated and depersonalizing technology, the universe has been transformed. The threat of extinction, psychic and physical, knocks daily on the door. The individual can be made to feel superfluous, without a destiny of his own. The constant menace of violence, destruction, and death on an unimaginable scale hangs over everyone, engendering apathy, if not despair, and often a spiritual vacuum, a persistent anguish and emptiness. Death has become the bedfellow.

The challenge, as I see it, is a coming to terms with life. At one point in his book, Herzog expresses a not dissimilar point of view: "The conscious attempt to enter into a genuine relationship with death has been prohibited in our age . . . by the fascination of science, since science has implicitly offered endless life, and so emptied both death and life of any true significance. The unconscious of modern man is not satisfied."

Where, then, does the contemporary analyst stand in relation to death, which has become invasive in a new way? I suggest that his most promising path is to focus on the personal, the inner death, and to nurture his patient's intrinsic value and his creative potential, thus hopefully transcending the ever-present threat from without which tends to reduce human capacity, perhaps dissolving the personality and causing collapse. Even though death will remain an undeniable aspect of existence that cannot be ignored, it need not be overwhelming. If a sense of helplessness threatens to overcome his patient, the analyst may attempt to open the way to a resur-

gence by helping to resuscitate the resources of the personal unconscious and the support that significant personal relationships, past
and present, can offer. Eventually, the numinous may become activated, intensifying spiritual fulfilment and an authentic sense of
personal identity. From a dull, empty silence, a healing, loving bond
with another may grow, giving an opportunity for unborn elements
of the self to develop. The key to becoming reconciled to death is to
be found in the quality of life.

Wunderli, Jürg. *Stirb und Werde: Wandlung und Wiedergeburt
in der Pubertät und in der Lebensmitte.* 1980. Pp. 154. Bonz,
pbk. (A free translation would read: *"Die and come to be
transformed. Rebirth in puberty and mid-life".*)

In a violence-ridden epoch, the sheer onslaught of a daily dose of
avoidable deaths may have ceased to outrage us, may have blunted
our sensibilities to the point of immunity. With this in mind, the title
of this interesting book should, perhaps, not be taken too pragmat-
ically.

Death, human mortality, has preoccupied mankind throughout
its history. The German title, *Stirb und Werde,* is borrowed from
Goethe's "Westöstlichen Diwan", written in an era very different
from our own. Goethe was concerned with the notion of metamorphosis, as symbolized, for instance, by the pupa ceasing to be
itself and becoming a moth. His writings preceded Darwin's theory
of evolution, of the survival of the fittest. His was a search for a
progression, "Steigung", as he called it, from the physical realities
to a spiritual dimension. There is common ground here with
Jung.

Butterflies and moths have been representations of the soul in
ancient myths. Thus, Goethe's poem anticipates Jung's warnings
about the potentially seductive nature of numinous, and so-called
spiritual, experience.

> "Then no distance holds you fast;
> winged, enchanted on you fly,
> light your longing, and at last
> moth, you meet the flame and die."

The subsequent stanza wholly accords with the author's theme:

> "Never prompted to that quest;
> die and dare rebirth!
> You remain a dreary guest
> on our gloomy earth."

This book's invitation to die so as to be reborn, and the implications thereof, need, in my view, to be taken both literally and intrapsychically, for the title could well be misleading to the layman, the more so if he has suicidal or homicidal propensities.

Furthermore, as readers of this volume will know only too well, disturbed and regressed patients associate quite minor changes, let alone separation experiences, with obliteration and death. Fear can overwhelm, blocking the progress to transformation with its ultimate goal, that of individuation, of death and rebirth. I find the author's unquestioning confidence that one inevitably flows from the other, as day follows night, over-optimistic, if not an idealization.

As to whether the reader will be confirmed and stimulated, or else incline towards querying the central thesis of Dr Wunderli's well-written book, will hinge on the nature of his own professional experiences, and on his personal philosophy, whereas the existentialists, for instance, hold that man should be deemed free and responsible. Clinicians working with borderline personality disorders and, more commonly, with patients relentlessly trapped in entrenched neurotic states, might be cautious about unreservedly equating subjective death experiences with personal growth, with transformation and rebirth. It could, at best, be irresponsible, even dangerous, to cling to such an assumption.

Any book that stimulates debate and controversy is to be welcome, though this one is somewhat diluted by its over-comprehensive inclusion of most of the current psychodynamic theories without a firm commitment to any one of them. This has turned it into something of a reviewer's nightmare, not unlike a dog with a buried bone.

The author, himself, describes his book as a guide, a kind of primer, signposting pertinent viewpoints while avoiding any firm alignment. By and large, however, Dr Wunderli has pitched his camp beyond Freud, closer to Jung, Erikson, and Mahler, in that he emphasizes the positive aspects of regression. He sees regression, perhaps somewhat one-sidedly, as a stimulus to progress and growth. He has painstakingly and ably documented two major confirmatory dream series. The first is on the death and rebirth theme; the second on the subject of individuation. These dream sequences do much to enhance and strengthen his thesis, and they highlight the writer's skill and erudition. It may well be that this rich feast will engender awe, envy, or incredulity in some. I think it may be crucial to consider whether regression and relapse are indistinguishable, which, it seems to me, is implied by the author. I cannot agree that they are. It is my impression that Dr Wunderli does not go far enough in sufficiently differentiating the one from the other. In my view, he asserts too confidently that a reversion of the libido to an earlier and more primitive stage of development is, *ipso facto*, an encounter with all the primary sources of creativity in the unconscious. Could it not be the case that some regressive states lead to acute suffering, to a sense of emptiness, despair, helplessness, and futility? I find the author has given too little credence to the tortuous regeneration from within which proceeds a positive outcome to regression.

On the topic of individuation, Dr Wunderli has incorporated Fordham's viewpoint without, however, giving any acknowledgement to his source. Furthermore, he goes beyond Jung's crucial views by specifying that an attainment of individuation presupposes the prior elimination of narcissistic disturbances, i.e., the under- and over-valuation of images of the self, a view with which I find myself wholly in accord. In this context, one cannot but agree that psychic development is subject to recurring experiences of loss and rediscovery. Furthermore, I see the attainment of individuation as an elusive goal, as the end of many converging journeys.

As implied by the sub-title, the book has two principle foci. The first is the period of puberty during which, it is postulated, the death–rebirth pattern is especially evident. The author argues that, if the child-like ego is abdicated in favour of an adult one, and is accompanied by the appropriate grief-work, a link may be forged between the ego and the self. I suggest that this is a lifetime's undertaking, which may precede, and certainly continues beyond, the age of puberty.

The other focal point on which the author concentrates is the mid-life period, a movable feast, I would say. Dr Wunderli stresses that man in mid-life is confronted with his limitations, and with his mortality. Surely, not only then! This all-important confrontation is described, rather poignantly, as "the highest autonomous achievement of the mature adult" and as "a renewed opportunity for a rebirth experience in which the dominance of the ego gives way to the self in the conscious process of individuation". At this point, the author concedes that the process of transformation during puberty and mid-life, as in the second half of life, are interdependent. "Any developmental evolution towards individuation cannot proceed until its previous stage has been completed." I am left wondering whether such an orderly chain of events reflects the ebb and flow of the living psyche and soma.

This book is to be recommended for the questions it raises, for its freshness, its lucid style, and its thought-provoking content.

Unedited communications from patients

A. T.

"Doesn't know who she is.

"On a day-to-day level she functions adequately. She runs a home, relates well to others and manages to do a part time job. At night she lies awake worrying about her performance on life's stage. Did she do or say the right thing? Is her boss thinking of giving her the order of the boot because A. is not able to decide what to do.

"The main thing she cares about is her family. She loves her husband but often feels he doesn't hear her. She loves her children but cannot find the right way to let them go. There are a few things she knows she does well. One of them is writing reports. That's why she has chosen to write in the third person, as an observer. A further reason for this strange choice is that she has been thinking a lot about a letter between a Hospital Physiatrist and a GP and concerning a resident she is working with. It contains three statements which are either untrue, inaccurate or doubtful. How can a mentally 'sick' person be healed? And what sets them apart from the healers? Sometimes she wonders whether she has more in common with the unhealed and their parents than with the carers. They, those resident patients with their long hospital history and their pills and their detailed knowledge of the spectrum of what the system is do not know who they are. Newspaper articles tell us that it is due to some biological–chemical factor or even partly determined by date of birth that they don't know who they are. (They do know that they are given a special role which perpetuates itself.) Those who have a psychodynamic view say no; it's backgrounds, parents' upbringing, early experience that make this group special. These parents—that must be where the key lies.

"I too am a parent. And I too am a child. What did I feel like when at the age of two and a half they sent me away to Miss M while my brother was born? And again when they sent me, aged nearly six to a holiday school because war broke out. Soon after there was a plan to send us to Canada which fell through. Meanwhile, they sent us to Wales. What did I feel like to be number six out of seven children, and how was it to carry the burden of the label "favourite". How didn't it feel to have a sister who broke down, broke up, broke? It sometimes seems that if I could remember those feelings I would know who I am.

"Eva once asked me some question about writing; was it more about doing something creative, imaginative or about trying to express this kind of stuff none of which is new?

"Doing something creative must be very therapeutic. I don't really have the urge to write or paint or sculpt or make music. These are really healthy things to do.

"It has some connection with one's fantasy life. I see myself as a very down - to - earth person not able to let go.

"This is a load of self-indulgent tripe. And I still wonder sometimes whether being in therapy is a self indulgence. What have I gained in over two years? (1) Reduction in anxiety. Better able to cope with it when it comes. I have missed Eva this month. Lots of bad nights. But it is liveable with.

"(2) Some insight into my dealing with others. (3) Sometimes a gain in confidence. For example I did want to get a job and managed to do so. The fact that it now causes me extra anxiety is something about change and movement. So it is not really a setback. Having a job was quite important to me for a number of reasons (a) money (b) status and (c) some structure to my time.

"Looking over what I have been writing, it strikes me as the ramblings of a very self-absorbed person—now I am going back to the third person reporting role. It's about someone who has almost got stuck in a time warp. The meaning of this is not quite clear.

"One more thing before I go back to bed—it is 2.45 a.m.—who am I writing for, me or Eva?

"I should like to study something but cannot decide what. Polish up my French, take Russian, a Jewish topic, something new and different, how about counselling?

"Which brings me back to my starting point. Who am I?"

B. L.

"It feels as if I've never been allowed to be carefree or have my parents really happy for me.

"They're 'happier' if you do as they want but not if you are happy as you, with no holes [sic] barred.

"Always to return to a place/building where he or she are there or both together and then it was the stress of (1) Arguments (2) Heart attacks (3) waking up in the night (4) Even glandular fever— they argued when I had a temperature of 103.4 and they argued and when they do/did it divided me inside—where was I in all of this— I felt bereft of any adults to stabilize me and my upset (emotions) struggled inside and feelings of being on my own and no one to help me. Sister never any company in all this.

"I feel now as if I'm still parenting or trying to win a body but that I'm too young to do it—that I wake up into this dream that is in fact reality and I suspect it to finish and me to be really elsewhere but I'm not sure where but I believe it is waking up and find I'm DEAD??

"There's a part of me always running scared of being still young and still wondering where my parents are—when they'll come and reassure me—tell me it was a test—tell me I'm ok—it's ok to feel and to panic and to fear . . . And to be lonely.

"It's when I'm not really here/there I struggle each day into the next and I almost forget or ignore or negate: that day/week/ month/year that has passed!!

"It's like one day somebody will tell me why I'm here and alive."

R. M.

"I thought it was a pity that you were unhappy about me booking appointments on an occasional basis as I felt this was just what I needed and could manage, and I thought from your point of view it enabled you to make use of sessions which would otherwise have gone to waste. I couldn't see what your other patients did had anything to do with it. This seemed an illogical thing to say and that is unusual for you. This made me wonder if it was what your training supervisor told you to do.

"Having read 'Talk is not enough—how psychotherapy really works' I must say I wasn't impressed by the people who taught the author, though he seemed to treat them as if they were infallible. I came to the conclusion that what he was taught was optimized to earn him a living rather than optimized to cure people, which is not the same thing although I don't think he could tell the difference.

"I've been thinking about why this treatment sometimes works and sometimes doesn't. One thing that struck me is the fact that the effect of school never seems to come into the equation.

"School teaches you all sorts of wrong ideas about how to deal with people without most people even realizing it, such as don't assert yourself, give the answer expected of you. If what you are telling people to do is in conflict with what they learn at school but this hasn't been dealt with. It will be more difficult for the patient to act on what he learns here, and it seems to me that it is only when thoughts and feelings lead to a change in behaviour that he is cured. Mary came up with an interesting thought when she said 'perhaps you are cured but you don't know what to do with your new cured self'.

"You've shown me what my problems with women are only too clearly. What I'm looking for now is to improve my people skills. I suppose I'd like some of the advantages of a private education without actually having had one! I don't see why this shouldn't be possible but I know it would mean unlearning much of what I learnt at school. I don't know if you could help me with this.

If I did manage to come once a week whilst I am working I would feel I was putting myself out for something that didn't really suit me and I would resent you for this, and from my experiences with AM I feel this would do me more harm than good. I know two friends who have excellent people skills and it would be safer to get them to give me some lessons.

"The last thing I want to do is make you unhappy, but I just thought it would be worth writing to say that if you ever change your mind about me having a session now and then, do let me know.

"Having told you what I thought was wrong with this treatment I've become very disillusioned with it.

"I know I came up with some good ideas but why was this necessary?

"Everyone knows school affects your personality, so why didn't someone in your profession think of this? Apart from training you not to assert yourself it teaches you to judge yourself by what others think of you. I'm sure this is the cause of a lot of shyness with women.

"And why didn't someone think of giving the patient exercises to do during the week?

"It seems to me that both these things are something which could be omitted from the treatment without the patient noticing, the first because everyone who has gone to school is affected in the same way, to different degrees, and therefore whatever faults they have are considered normal, and the second because the patient probably views the treatment in the same light as going to the dentist so he does not expect this.

"It seems to me that the treatment has evolved to have the maximum chance of failing, or at least last as long as possible, without the patient being aware of it.

"On reflection I feel it was naive of me to expect anything else. I once worked on a project, which was a "costs plus" contract. The longer they took to do the job the more money they made. I was there three weeks before my boss gave me any work to do!

"I thought you were someone who had been trained to deal with any problem but it seems I've ended up teaching you. I'm sure you do the very best you can but it doesn't say much for your training, does it?

"If I bought an electric kettle, I wouldn't expect to put a new element in it before I could use it.

"By the same token, I would like to ask for a partial refund on the grounds that the analysis provided was not suitable for the purposes intended.

"However I'll leave it up to you to decide whether you think this is fair or not. If you don't then I'll leave it at that.

"The last few weeks have been quite difficult for me, in that I feel I have been let down both by the educational system and by yourself. Perhaps things haven't been easy for you either.

"It was more by luck than by judgement that I came up with some of my ideas. I was thinking about my girlfriend, and wishing I could be confident with people like she is when I asked myself the question 'What's stopping me?' which led to many of my ideas.

"The thing I don't like about this treatment most, however, is the way they try to indoctrinate you into coming every week. Ludovic Kennedy said he went to a therapist for twenty-three years. As far as I could see he was just as miserable at the end of it as he was at the start. There but for the grace of God go I, I think to myself,

"At least I stood a better chance with you than with anyone else, however, which is one thing I can be grateful for.

"Maybe your book will shake things up a bit. I do hope so. As it stands, I think if psychotherapy was a horse, I'd shoot it to put it out of its misery, and I believe most of the public would too!

"I don't think I'm going to be very good company on Friday. Perhaps you can cheer me up, you never know. I hope you are well . . ."

REFERENCES

Abelin, E. L. (1975). Some further observations and comments on the earliest role of the father. *International Journal of Psychoanalysis, 56*(3).

Balint, M. (1968). *The Basic Fault.* London: Tavistock.

Barcal, A. (1971). Family therapy in the treatment of anorexia nervosa. *American Journal of Psychiatry, 128*(3).

Barker, C. (1972). *Healing in Depth.* London: Hodder & Stoughton.

Bruch, H. (1974). *Eating Disorders and the Person Within.* London: Routledge & Kegan Paul.

Crisp, A. H., Harding, B., & McGuiness, B. (1974). Anorexia nervosa—psychoneurotic characteristics of parents: relations to prognosis. A quantitative study. *Journal of Psychosomatic Research, 18*(3):

Eliot, T. S. (1925). *Poems 1909–1925.* London: Faber & Faber.

Eliot, T. S. (1940). East Coker. In: *Four Quartets.* London: Faber & Faber.

Fordham, M. (1969). *Children as Individuals.* London: Hodder & Stoughton.

Fordham, M. (1971). Primary self, primary narcissism and related concepts. *Journal of Analytical Psychology, 16*(2).

Fordham, M. (1980). The emergence of child analysis. *Journal of Analytical Psychology, 25*(4).

Galdston, R. (1974). Mind over matter: observations on 50 patients hospitalized with anorexia nervosa. *Journal of the American Academy of Child Psychiatry, 13*(2).

Greenacre, P. (1966). Problems of over-idealization of the analyst and of the analysis. *Psychoanalytic Study of the Child, 21.*

Henderson, D. K., & Gillespie, R. D. (1969). *Textbook of Psychiatry* (10th revised edn). Oxford: Oxford University Press.

Jung, C. G. (1926). Analytical psychology and education. *C.W., 17.*

Jung, C. G. (1933). The real and the surreal. *C.W., 8.*

Jung, C. G. (1935). *The Tavistock Lectures. C.W., 18.*

Jung, C. G. (1940). The psychology of the child archetype. *C.W., 9:* 1. London: Routledge & Kegan Paul.

Jung, C. G. (1942). A psychological approach to the Trinity. *C.W., 11.* London: Routledge & Kegan Paul.

Jung, C. G. (1946). The psychology of the transference. *C.W., 16.* London: Routledge & Kegan Paul.

Jung, C. G. (1953). *Psychology and Alchemy, C.W., 12.* London: Routledge & Kegan Paul.

Jung, C. G. (1963). *Memories, Dreams, Reflections.* London: Collins and Routledge & Kegan Paul.

Kierkegaard, S. (1983). *Kierkegaard's Writings, Vol. 9. Fear & Trembling Repetition.* Princeton University Press.

Kohut, H. (1977). *The Restoration of the Self.* New York: International Universities Press.

Lawrence, D. H. (1962). *The Collected Letters. Vol. I.* H. T. Moore (Ed.). London: Heinemann.

Lawrence, D. H. (1933). *Selected Poems.* The Poetry Bookshelf.

Layland, W. R. (1981). In search of a loving father. *International Journal of Psychoanalysis, 62*(2).

Liebman, R., Minuchin, S., & Baker, L. (1974). The role of the family in the treatment of anorexia nervosa. *Journal of the American Academy of Child Psychiatry, 13*(2).

Mahler, M. S., Pine, F., & Bergman, A. (1975). *The Psychological Birth of the Human Infant.* London: Hutchinson.

Meier, C. A. (1963). Psycho-somatic medicine from the Jungian point of view. *Journal of Analytical Psychology, 8*(2).

Newton, K. (1981). Comment on "The emergence of child analysis", by M. Fordham. *Journal of Analytical Psychology, 26*(1).

Newton, K., & Redfearn, J. (1977). The real mother, ego–self relations and personal identity. *Journal of Analytical Psychology, 22*(4).

Plaut, A. (1959). Hungry patients. *Journal of Analytical Psychology, 4*(2).

Rolandi, E., Azzolini, A., & Barabino, A. (1973). Present possibilities of neuroendocrinal study in anorexia nervosa. Report of a clinical case. *Archives E. Maragliano, 29*(1).

Scharf, R. (1967). *Satan in the Old Testament.* Evanston: North-Western University Press.

Schenck, K., & Deegener, G. (1974). Therapy of anorexia nervosa. *Medizinische Welt, 25*(24).

Searles, H. F. (1961). The sources of anxiety in paranoid schizophrenia. *British Journal of Medical Psychology, 34*(2).

Seligman, E. (1976). A psychological study of anorexia nervosa. *Journal of Analytical Psychology, 21*(2): 193

Seligman, E. (1982). The half-alive ones. *Journal of Analytical Psychology, 27*(1): 1.

Thompson, E. (Ed.). (1981). *Social Trends.* Government Statistical Services, No. 11. London: HMSO.

Wilke, H.-J. (1971). Problems in heart neurosis. *Journal of Analytical Psychology, 16*(2).

Wilson, A. T. M. (1949). Some reflections and suggestions on the prevention of marital problems. *Human Relations, 2*: 233–251.

INDEX